ACTIVISTIC ROLE OF PENCRAFT
IN
NATION BUILDING

BY

DR. DAMINABO SONNY BRIGGS

Published in Nigeria by:
Osia Digital Press
#8 Owhonda Street,
Mile 3 Diobu Port Harcourt.
Rivers State.
Tel: 08033128938, 08037085272.

Email: lillianclinic@gmail.com

DEDICATION

This book is dedicated to all God-fearing journalists, human rights activists and the multi-dimensionally poor Nigerians.

ACKNOWLEDGEMENT

To God be the glory!

CONTENTS

<u>ACRONYMS</u>

NC	-	National Conference
HIV	-	Human Immunodeficiency Virus
AID	-	Acquired Immunodeficiency Syndrome
PPPRA	-	Petroleum Products Pricing and Regulatory Agency
NNPC	-	Nigerian National Petroleum Corporation
NLC	-	Nigeria Labour Congress
NEPA	-	National Electric Power Authority
NDDC	-	Niger Delta Development Commission
PRONACO	-	Pro-National Conference Organization
INEC	-	Independent National Electoral Commission
AC	-	Action Congress
PDP	-	Peoples Democratic Party
APC	-	All Progressives Congress
NDBDA	-	Niger Delta Basin Development Authority
OMPADEC	-	Oil Mineral Producing Areas Development Commission
PTF	-	Petroleum Trust Fund
PHCN	-	Power Holding Company of Nigeria
TI	-	Transparency International
EFCC	-	Economic and Financial Crimes Commission
ICPC	-	Independent Corrupt Practices and Other Related Offences Commission
LGs	-	Local Governments
LGAs	-	Local Government Areas
ACF	-	Arewa Consultative Forum
SAN	-	Senior Advocate of Nigeria

US	-	United States
CPI	-	Corruption Perception Index
GCI	-	Global Competitiveness Index
WEF	-	World Economic Forum
HDI	-	Human Development Index
UNDP	-	United Nations Development Program
UK	-	United Kingdom
RMAFC	-	Revenue Mobilization Allocation and Fiscal Commission
ISBN	-	International Standard Book Number
ISSN	-	International Standard Serial Number
GCFR	-	Grand Commander of the Order of the Federal Republic
DMO	-	Debt Management Office
PVC	-	Permanent Voters Card
PVCs	-	Permanent Voters Cards
SUVs	-	Sport Utility Vehicles

INTRODUCTION

The exposition of my triadic nature is a humbling experience: from a lowly beginning as a mathematician to an Obstetrician Gynaecologist and a writer.

I thank the LORD GOD ALMIGHTY for giving me the innate ability and the flair to write.

Other books I have written include:

- ✓ AZ Mafia – The Namerian Experience (A novel, 2002)
- ✓ Reincarnation and the concept of being born again (2002)
- ✓ HIV/AIDS – The gateway to Prevention (2003)
- ✓ The King and his Slaves (A Play, 2006)
- ✓ How to fight corruption in Nigeria (2011)
- ✓ The Problem with Nigeria (2014)
- ✓ A Potpourri of Poems (2017)
- ✓ The Awesomeness of God (2020)
- ✓ The Wonders of God in my Life (2024)

I have also written many articles and commentaries, some of which had been published in Nigerian Newspapers and Magazines.

The idea or spirit behind my 'pen-activities' is to convey to the world the feelings of the voiceless people clamouring for good governance, responsive and responsible leadership, equity and justice.

The idea is also to critically appraise the activities of Government; and laud or criticize constructively when necessary, with a view to contributing to National Development and Growth. This is the kernel of good journalistic practice. It enables the authorities gauge their performances, democratic dividends and leadership style.

The question of failure of leadership in Nigeria was discussed by the erudite and iconic Late Professor, Chinua Achebe, in his short book titled, **"The Trouble with Nigeria"**, 1983. I made reference to it in my own short book of similar or identical title, **"The Problem with Nigeria"**, 2014.

Permit me to quote from this sage:
"The trouble with Nigeria is simply and squarely a failure of leadership. There is nothing basically wrong with the Nigerian character. There is nothing wrong with the Nigerian land or climate or water or air or anything else. The Nigerian problem is the unwillingness or inability of its leaders to rise to the responsibility, to the challenge of personal example which are the hallmarks of true leadership."

How will the leadership not fail when the processes of recruitment are faulty? How will it not fail when personal, ethnic or regional considerations are considered over and above the national interests? How will it not fail when we worship corruption as our god? How will it not fail when we become so adapted to nepotistic behaviour and hidden and not-so-hidden agendas?

How do we now solve the problem of recurrent leadership failure in Nigeria? Let us for a moment cast our minds back to what happened in South Africa's Apartheid governance and the agitations led by the Late icon and sage, Nelson Rolihlahla Mandela. Mandela was offered to lead the Apartheid regime during the negotiations but he bluntly refused. He opined that leadership or good leadership was not going to solve the apartheid imbroglio in South Africa without tampering with the <u>Structure</u> or Constitution of the country. It was only after a **New Constitution** came into place that he agreed to participate in the post-apartheid politics.

Thankfully, with deep thinking and the unassailable and shining example from the South African case, the solution to our recurrent leadership failures has been proffered as highlighted in my 2014 book, titled, "The Problem with Nigeria".

And the solution is simple– restructure Nigeria. A new Constitution is a sine qua non, just like in South Africa.

Please permit me to quote what I wrote in my 2014 book:
"The problem with Nigeria", page vi and vii: "The problem with Nigeria is the fault in its structure. There is nothing significant any superhuman can do in leadership. Even if we bring Angels from Mars, Jupiter or Neptune to rule us, no significant progress will be made with the present way Nigeria is constituted".

The conclusion then and now is that the failure of leadership in Nigeria is as a result of the structural defects of the Nigerian foundation. What we are experiencing now: the degree and ferocity of the violence, insecurity and the killings will even worsen if the country is not restructured quickly, along True Federalism.

What drives my passion to write against injustice is innate in me because right from my childhood I had been a hater of injustice, a lover and embracer of fairness, equality and justice.

"Do to others what you expect them to do to you" should be the golden rule in our day-to-day activities, and also in our politics! Constructive criticisms are the hallmarks of patriotic citizenship especially when things are going awry.

Keeping quiet or taking a neutral stance when the country is 'burning' is a great sin or crime against humanity.
This narrative is corroborated by quotes from many sages:

✓ "To sin by silence when they should protest makes cowards of men"- **Ella Wheeler Wilcox**

✓ "If you are neutral in situations of injustice you have chosen the side of the oppressor. If an elephant has its foot on the tail of a mouse and you say that you are neutral, the mouse will not appreciate your neutrality.
- **Archbishop Desmond Tutu**

✓ "A man dies when he refuses to stand up for that which is right. A man dies when he refuses to stand up for justice. A man dies when he refuses to take a stand for that which is true".- **Dr. Martin Luther King Jr.**

✓ "As long as poverty, injustice and gross inequality persist in our world, none of us can truly rest".- **Nelson Mandela**

✓ "Where you see wrong or inequality or injustice, speak out because this is your country. This is your democracy. Make it. Protect it. Pass it on".- **Thurgood Marshall**

✓ "Silence becomes cowardice when occasion demands speaking out the whole truth and acting accordingly".
- **Mahatma Gandi**

ü "The ultimate tragedy is not the oppression and cruelty by the bad people but the   silence over that by the   good people"-   **Dr. Martin Luther King Jr.**

✓ "Injustice anywhere is a threat to justice everywhere".
-        **Martin Luther King Jr.**

✓ "First they came for the <u>socialists</u>, and I did not speak out-because I was not a socialist. Then they came for the <u>trade unionists,</u> and I did not speak out – because I was not a trade unionist. Then they came for the <u>Jews,</u> and I did not speak out- because I was not a Jew. Then they came for me – and there was no one left to speak for me".
-        **German Pastor, Martin Niemoller**

✓ "The world will not be destroyed by those who do evil, but by those who watch them without doing anything".- **Albert Einstein**

I have, over the decades, written many useful, riveting articles to drive the agenda, armed with boundless enthusiasm and deep seated passion for the welfare and service of our people to enjoy good governance and live in peace, harmony and happiness. Many of such articles had been published in reputable Newspapers and Magazines.

Some of the articles still in my possession are hereby reproduced verbatim, each being followed by comments, fuelled by prevailing circumstances and current positive thinking.

FREQUENT FUEL PRICE HIKES AS DIVIDENDS OF DEMOCRACY
PUBLISHED BY THE MIRROR, 2005

The essence of good leadership and true democracy is to serve the best interests of the majority of the people. When this basic ingredient suffers pathological lack in a body politic, the people are doomed to suffer!

And to say the truth, we deserve what we are getting. No one should complain if fuel prices are hiked on weekly basis as local prices are tied to global best practices. Nemesis is gradually creeping in for the complacent, cowardly and gullible Nigerians who are known to be notoriously lackadaisical. And since the ruling class has detected this trait in us, would anyone blame them for taking advantage of it?

The hardship, joblessness, insecurity, collapsed economy etc. we face today are the prices we have to pay for our timidity and carelessness. We fought the military and eventually installed a civilian government that is not better than the military. Well-meaning Nigerians like Chief Gani Fawehinimi and Chief Odumegu Ojukwu among others warned us of the dangers ahead. What do you expect from a party that allegedly did not win in any State as exemplified in Ogun and Anambra States. If the President did not win his own State, where else could he win? When we allow rigging to take place we should not

complain about misrule and the suffering of the masses.
President Obasanjo has succeeded in increasing fuel price for a record-breaking nine times from May 1999 to date. If we are alive to our responsibilities, we should call for solutions from the Minister for Petroleum. Incidentally, the President is also the Minister for Petroleum. It was just few weeks ago he appointed Dr. Daukoru as Minister of State to assist him.

All of a sudden, they have craftily introduced terms such as Independent Marketers, Petroleum Products Pricing and Regulatory Agency (PPPRA) to confuse the masses in the handling of oil issues. The blame for frequent hikes is now shifted to such bodies and not the Government as it appears to wash its hands off. The questions one may ask are: is there no Government in Nigeria again? Is Government dead or powerless as to allow a body like PPPRA, which was set up by the Government, behave like colossus bestriding the country and crushing the citizens to extinction? Why is Government shirking its responsibilities? Who are the members of PPPRA and independent marketers? Are they Nigerians? Do they live in Nigeria? Are they blind to the sufferings of the people? Why are they supporting such outrageous increase in this critical time? Is Government also oblivious of the plight of the people? Are we all deaf to the cries of the people because of profit in dollars?
True or false, people are alleging that the craze for the frequent increases in fuel price is because all the filling stations in Nigeria have been bought over by powerful people.

The hackneyed and recurring reasons for the incessant fuel

price hikes are untenable and baseless. Sample some of them: The international price of a barrel of oil has increased and that we have to pay at the international rate since they import at the same rate. Since the watchword is deregulation, there is no going back as stated by the President himself.

If what we are seeing and experiencing is what is meant by deregulation, which sole aim is to strangulate the populace, then let us do away with 'deregulation' right now. If we must buy petroleum products at international rate, then we must stop all oil explorations in Nigeria because the masses are not benefiting from such huge sales.

Why is it that Government is selectively mouthing and applying international rates when it comes to sale of fuel to the citizens? Why not apply same international rates to salary payments, social services and other sundry benefits enjoyed by citizens abroad? Government, therefore, should endeavour to pay our salaries in Dollars and Pound Sterling as it is done for the Finance Minister and others in the cabinet. If this can't be done, then we should be paid equivalent amount in Naira, enabling us to pay up to N200, N300 per litre of fuel.
The snag in this is that majority of the people will still be in deep valley of poverty and misery as the working class in Nigeria is less than 0.0001% of our population, considering the mass retrenchment that is being planned to take place soon.

Another reason for the incessant fuel price hikes is that of subsidy. That is that the NNPC and invariably the Federal Government of Nigeria cannot afford to subsidise for the consumption of fuel. No one is impressed by this subsidy issue. Removal of so-called subsidy started two to three decades ago and we are still subsidising. If it is true that in spite of the excess money from crude oil we cannot continue to sustain subsidy then, we are in for trouble.

Another much touted reason for this sorry pass is the non-functioning of our refineries, necessitating importation of fuel. President Obasanjo early in his first term, pumped in millions of dollars to revitalise Kaduna Refinery. Millions of dollars were alleged to go down the drain in the name of maintenance; millions of dollars that could have built two to three giant refineries. The reason why government is not interested in building new refineries or repairing existing ones may just be to favour their chosen marketers, children, relatives and cronies to reap huge profits from oil importation to the detriment of the masses.

One other nauseating argument, framed by agents of Government is to compare the price of a litre of fuel in Dahomey with what is obtained here in Nigeria. According to them, a litre of fuel sells for N105 in Dahomey, so why should Nigerians complain if government is magnanimous enough to sell the same litre of fuel for N70 in Nigeria? These same agents fail to mention places where fuel is almost free for their citizens such as Qatar and Saudi Arabia. Even in neighbouring Ghana, which has no oil, fuel is less expensive than in Nigeria.

The fact that Government is adamantly opposed to reversal of the hike to its former price of N51.50 shows that it initiated the incessant increases through NNPC and the marketers.

In a true democracy where you have checks and balances, the Legislature can't sit quietly while the Executive continues to have its way. From 1999 till date, Government has hiked fuel prices nine times. What has the Legislature done to stop this trend in the last six years? Nothing. At best, they would oppose any hike by making feeble noise in the morning only to share the "dividends" of the price hike with the Executive in the afternoon! What came out from the Mantu Committee set up by the President some months ago to put a stop to incessant price hikes? Nothing!! Now, the Legislature is waking up from sleep to pass a bill to stabilise fuel price after it has been hiked to between N70 to N100 per litre! What a shame!

We cannot boast of strong labour unions whose principled stands can be bought over with diamond and gold. The current price hike was long in coming but the NLC did nothing except to say it is a joke until it became a reality. A committed NLC would have matched propaganda for propaganda, and action for action. Mobilisation would have been thorough enough to declare action immediately filling stations adjusted their metres. The idea of waiting for one month for negotiations and dialogue is just playing into the mouth of a hungry lion! Or is it a special arrangement with the Executive to wait for the new prices to stabilise and the people forced to swallow the bitter pill before making some noise? In the midst of the noise the price will now "come down" from N70 per litre to N69.50 per litre!

The right and proper thing to do in the long-term is for the Government to build modern refineries immediately and stop importation of fuel. Government cannot say they don't have the money to build refineries. The cost of crude oil in 1999 was $16/barrel, now it is $66/barrel. So the $50 difference or so per barrel of oil sold multiplied by number of barrels produced since 1999 till date should be used to finance construction of new refineries and maintenance of existing ones.

Comments

This article on incessant fuel price hikes was written way back in 2005. Nineteen years down the line, it is deja vu and even worse now with fuel selling more than N600 per litre!

I painstakingly analysed the problems and gave lasting solutions as a patriot. Nobody listened! We have had four different sets of Government since 2005 till date but nothing changed. In fact, the problems multiplied and the hardships became worse!

There is something fundamentally wrong with Nigeria. The fault is the structure! To cure is to restructure!

THE MANY 'SINS' OF THE PEOPLE OF THE NIGER DELTA IN CUSTODY AND IN GRAVES

PUBLISHED BY THE MIRROR, 2005

The Almighty Creator created the Niger Delta with its difficult terrain: mangrove forests, swamps and creeks. The same Almighty Creator created the 'black gold' beneath the difficult terrain to help the people develop their environment. How great are His wondrous works, using the oil as a tool to drive the 'flies off the backs of tailless animals'!

The Almighty Creator is not mocked. To overturn His glorious plans and turn them to perpetual curse and tragedy for the people of the Niger Delta is a burden too great for the people to bear.

The peace-loving people of the Niger Delta had endured for more than half a century what other communities anywhere in the world would not be able to tolerate for half a second! Each indigene of the Niger Delta has, vicariously, committed a sin; and that is the fact of being born in the Niger Delta. And the original sin clones numerous other sins with dangerous dimensions and complications.

The Niger Delta was (and is) not a conquered territory, not even by the British! The Willink's Minority Commission elaborated on the protection of minority rights in Nigeria and set guidelines for their developmental goals. But that is not even the point.

The people of the Niger Delta love Nigeria even to a piteous fault. They are selfless individuals, ready to give out to other people what they lack! The people of the Niger Delta are not even envious of the monumental developments oil has brought to other parts of Nigeria. Take Lagos for an example. Look at the infrastructure in Lagos, the beautiful bridges. And now Abuja! Look at the magnificent buildings and the super-structures, the roads. Where did they get the money to develop Abuja, if not from oil in the Niger Delta? Abuja is being developed without setting up any Commission like NDDC in the Niger Delta. Don't the people of the Niger Delta need modern bridges from Port Harcourt to Nembe, from Port Harcourt to Bonny, from Port Harcourt to Bakana and Isaka, connecting Tombia, Bukuma to Buguma? Why can't we connect Borokiri to Okrika, Degema to Ogonokom, Agada and even get to Kula, why not? In decades past, there was Abonnema seaport. Why is this seaport not resuscitated? Why is it that NEPA grid has not yet been connected to Bayelsa State? Why is it that NEPA grid cannot reach places like Bakana, Abonnema, Bukuma and other motorable places? Why is it that most of the roads in the Southern parts of Nigeria are impassable and thus serve as death-traps? Why is it that the Uniport bridge is not dualised? Many accidents had occurred there. Are we waiting for it to collapse before we do anything, our usual 'fire-brigade' method? Industry road in Port Harcourt is an eyesore. And this is the first road that the foreigner sees as he arrives Port Harcourt seaport!

The people of the Niger Delta are visited with all kinds of punishment for their 'sin' of being born in such territory. Fishing and farming which used to be their natural occupations are no longer thriving due to oil pollution. Their environment has been denuded, degraded and destroyed. Oil companies that should serve as succour to the poverty-stricken indigenes are mainly controlled by others, dictating who should be employed or sacked and even dictating who should be given scholarships meant for the indigenes!

Let us look at Oloibiri where oil was first struck in Nigeria in 1956. What did Oloibiri and the people of Oloibiri gain from the billions of dollars sucked out from that region? Oloibiri is left desolate and abandoned, compare Oloibiri with Abuja? **With tears surging and clouding the writer's view, let us pause for the reader's response!**

The people of the Niger Delta are not asking for the sky! Take 75% of their oil and give them, a mere 25% for now. It this too much? Look at the billions of dollars stashed in foreign banks allegedly by General Sanni Abacha. The writer expected this money to be set aside for the development of the Niger Delta just as it is done for Abuja. After all, the money came from the Region.

The heroes of our past should not be forgotten.
Major Isaac Adaka Boro fought for the liberation of the people of the Niger Delta. He frowned at the magnitude of injustice meted out to the people of the Niger Delta. He wanted to put a stop to the siphoning of their God-given oil in return for nothing.

Same with Ken Saro Wiwa. He was very vocal in his nonviolent agitation for justice for the people of the Niger Delta, especially the Ogonis. He internationalised the struggle for the emancipation of his people.

<u>Comments</u>

Nineteen years or so after this article was written and published, the people of the Niger Delta are now visited with more devastating 'tragedies' than in 2005. Poverty, joblessness and marginalisation have all been multiplied; the despoliation of the environment has quadrupled. Fishing and farming, the mainstay of our occupation, are virtually nonexistent with recurrence of oil pollution of our lands and seas. The pollution is made worse by the very old and rusted pipelines, laid more than sixty years ago without replacement, and the craze for bursting the pipelines in pursuit of illegal oil refining.

The widespread pollution and the constant gas flaring in the Niger Delta lead to environmental degradation, resulting in high incidence of cancers, respiratory complications, hunger and deaths.

WHAT NIGERIA NEEDS IS NOT CONSTITUTIONAL AMENDMENT

PUBLISHED BY THE HARD TRUTH, 2006

Playing and replaying this old "gramophone song" of Constitutional amendment or the clone of it to Nigerians, and its ready acceptance of this hackneyed tune by Nigerians, shows that we do not understand the real problem of Nigeria and how to go about solving it! And that is why anyone can easily manipulate us. Why is it that we forget so easily? Why is it that we don't learn from our mistakes, why is it that the masses are so gullible?

Former President (Ibrahim) Babangida and late General Sani Abacha came up with their Constitutional amendments. Nothing came out from such gatherings, and we lost Billions of Naira organising such jamborees. (Gen.) Abdulsalami Abubakar came up with our present Constitution, 1999, and President Olusegun Obasanjo swore to defend the Constitution that he had not seen with his *"crowcrow"* eyes! And now, President Obasanjo wants to give us a New Constitution, which is pregnant with the alleged third-term project few hours to the end of his tenure!!

What Nigeria needs is not constitutional amendment. We have gone beyond that. Nigeria has had series of constitutions right from the 1950s. Getting a good Constitution has never been our problem, but just like anything in Nigeria, it is the implementation that is troublesome. So why is the Government throwing away

Billions of our oil money in the name of amendment?
What Nigeria needs to move forward is to listen and take the advice of our most respected sage, Late Chief Obafemi Awolowo who argued very convincingly that for Nigeria to make progress, each ethnic Nationality should be autonomous and be allowed to develop at its own pace.

This is to say that we need to restructure Nigeria along the path of True Federalism and do away with the Unitary System.

To move Nigeria forward, there is compelling need to grant autonomy to ethnic groups within the umbrella of a United Nigeria. These ethnic groups will control their resources and pay appropriate taxes to the centre for the general upkeep and good governance of the country. Anything short of this will make us move in endless circles without any progress. If Nigeria will survive, then we need to restructure the country now.

Invitation has been thrown to the public for presentations and submissions from the six geopolitical zones to amend the Constitution.

This is a monumental waste of the people's funds, grand deceit and a merry-go-round, loaded with alleged hidden third-term agenda.

Looking at developments from the geopolitical zones, some are ready to boycott the Constitutional amendment while others are busy jotting down their demands. But these demands have been discussed during the National Political Reforms Conference, even though some sore points were left untouched. Why are we thus repeating ourselves again and again without taking any action on previous conferences?

If we are to make progress, we should stop this Constitutional Amendment and encourage Nigerians to participate in the PRONACO Conference. This will benefit Nigeria as it will lead to restructuring of the system.

We have problems in Nigeria largely because we are docile and gullible. These are, invariably, the products of ignorance, poverty and illiteracy.

If constitutional amendment is the way to go, then we should push for:

1.   **Abrogation of Land Use Act and Petroleum Act or Decree.**
2.   **Abolition of the Skewed Representations in the House of Representatives.**
3.   **Abolition of the Skewed Local Government Areas.**
4.   **Fairness in Distribution of States:** Nigeria is divided into Six Zones for geo-political reasons, namely: North West, North Central, North East, South West, South South and South East. The South East has only five States compared with other zones that have six or seven States!

5.   **Fairness in REVENUE ALLOCATION:** The current revenue allocation is unfair and unjust. The clamour, mainly from the Niger Delta, is to adopt the 50% derivation that was used in the past when groundnut, palm oil and cocoa were holding sway.

6.   **POWER SHIFT:** If we adopt true federalism and resource control, there will be no need to fight for control of the centre.

In conclusion, what Nigeria needs is not an amended Constitution but the WILL to do what is right for Nigeria and Nigerians. And that is to re-structure the country along True Federalism in the strict sense of it. To achieve that, we need to sit down and dialogue as canvassed by PRONACO, reach agreement or consensus and then subject the resolution to a free and fair referendum. Then a truly new Constitution will emerge.

Comments

Recall that this article was written and published in 2006. The fact that the Nigerian question has been lingering over the decades is not because our leaders were or are bereft of the knowledge to do what is right; but because our leaders were /are maximally benefiting from the undue advantages of the status quo.

Of course, no sensible person(s) will blame those who are enjoying greater benefits from the lopsided allocation of resources. After all, no one will say 'don't give me more'. The fault is not with anyone of us. The fault is in the system we are running.

So, a restructured Nigeria holds a better, brighter, peaceful, progressive and harmonious country for all irrespective of religion or ethnicity. The status quo i.e. Unitary system, we are operating has no future for Nigerians, not even for the children of those who are enjoying it now.

Moreover, all of us stand to benefit more from a restructured Nigeria because of numerous unmined solid minerals that abound in the North and other regions of Nigeria.

THE FORTHCOMING 2007 ELECTIONS

PUBLISHED BY THE HARD TRUTH, 2006

The writer, a patriot with zero party affiliation, is very much surprised that Nigerians especially the opposition parties, notably ANPP, AC and others are quite comfortable and do not see anything wrong with the President appointing or nominating the INEC Chairman as head arbiter or referee in the forthcoming 2007 elections.

It is probably only in Nigeria where a President who is a very vocal PDP party member will appoint an umpire who is to organise a free and fair election! Of course, in spite of what others think, the chairman is most likely to dance to the tune of his master. Remember, he who pays the piper dictates the tune!

The writer is shocked to his bone marrow to observe that none of the opposition parties is making any consistent and persistent challenge to this illegality. One begins to wonder whether PDP has surreptitiously implanted their members into key positions in the ANPP, AC and other opposition parties. Or is it that all other parties have been hypnotised, bought over with money or intimidated?

The **Chief Electoral Officer** in any credible Commission should be appointed or selected by general consensus of all the leading political parties and not by a President, who is a jealous participant in the election process.

The closest analogy one can draw is to imagine PDP as a football team playing a world cup final with the opposition party as opponents. **What result do you expect from such a match with PDP member as the referee?** The funny but annoying fact is that the parties have not yet seen the handwriting on the wall and are taking things for granted!

The 'must-win' attitude, otherwise called 'do-or-die politics' is evidenced by the insistence of the Presidency appointing the INEC Chairman in an election, the Presidency himself is going to be a participant!

The political parties in Nigeria must therefore devise a system or process to deny the President exercising the power to appoint the INEC Chairman, who is the sole arbiter in elections; such appointments should be by consensual agreement by all parties.

Comments

Many factors determine the credibility and fairness of the conduct of elections. One of which is the appointment of the arbiter, who is the INEC Chairman. Situations where the President of a country is involved in the appointment process of the arbiter cannot be said to be free and fair, for obvious incontestable reasons.

I was really surprised that the opposition parties in 2006 did not even raise any eyebrows and allowed the President then (Chief Obasanjo) to so appoint Iwu as INEC Chairman. PDP continued on this warped notion until it was swept away by APC. The ruling party, APC, too is enjoying the maximum benefit from this anomaly while the PDP and other political parties doze off!

It is never too late to right the wrongs. The INEC Chairman and all Commissioners should not be appointed by any President or party in power to man our elections. It should be done by general consensus of all parties, to allow a level-playing field for all.

The best option open to us is to adopt or implement Justice Uwais Report on Electoral Reforms.

RESOLVING THE NIGER DELTA CRISIS: WHAT MANNER OF MASTER PLAN?

PUBLISHED BY THE MIRROR, 2007

The Niger Delta crisis has lingered on because successive Governments had only paid lip service to the plight of the region. If Government is genuinely sincere and willing to resolve the crisis in the region it can be done.

So if the Government of President Yar'adua and Goodluck Jonathan is poised to make a paradigm shift in favour of the people of the Niger Delta, we welcome it. The release of Alhaji Asari Dokubo is the right step on the road map for the emancipation of the Niger Deltans. 'Yanka dede' to President Yar'adua and goodluck to Goodluck Jonathan!

The history of the Niger Delta and the heroic struggles of our people are well-known to all, locally and internationally. There is no need to reel out the concatenation of events but suffice it to state the salient points as foundational basis for this article.

The fear of alienation, marginalization and oppression of the Niger Delta by the majority tribes necessitated the setting up of the Sir Henry Willink Commission in 1957. The Commission recommended a Federal Board to look into the problems of the Niger Delta; so Niger Delta Development Board was set up by Parliamentary Act in 1961. Subsequently, Niger Delta Basin Development Authority (NDBDA) was set up with full powers to develop the Niger Delta according to the guidelines set by the Willink Commission.

This, on the surface, would ordinarily bring smiles to the faces of the

people of the Niger Delta. But this was never to be! The NDBDA
did not perform optimally because it was not adequately funded.

   The setting up seemed to be a façade to give the impression that
something was being done to address the problems of the Niger
Delta, whereas the opposite was the case.

The scuttling of the advantages and benefits that should accrue to
the people of the Niger Delta is still continuing till today.
The 1.5% Derivation fund was grudgingly set up to try to give a
human face to the masquerade of injustice. Before the Nigerian
Civil War, Derivation Fund was on the principle of 50%. Why
reduce this principle of derivation to mere 1.5%?
As was expected, the 1.5% Derivation Fund could not help
matters. Further agitation pushed the Derivation Fund to 13%,
which fell far short of the 50% demanded by the people of the Niger
Delta. Regrettably, nobody from the Niger Delta knows quite
accurately the actual number of barrels of crude oil lifted from the
shores of the Niger Delta on daily basis. So, the question is 13% of
what? When we do not know the actual total number of barrels of
oil lifted, how can we calculate the 13%? Hence the so-called
increase from 1.5% Derivation to 13% Derivation without
knowing the correct total can be misleading! With relevant
manipulative arithmetic, the 13% Derivation could even be far
less than the former 1.5% Derivation. Verify this simple
calculation:
1.5% of 1,950,000 barrels of oil   =   29,250 barrels
13% of 1,950 barrels of oil   =   2,535 barrels
With this revelation, it is now easy to understand the possibility of
exploitation, cheating and outright stealing in the last fifty years
(when oil was first struck in Oloibiri in 1956).

Oil Mineral Producing Areas Development Commission (OMPADEC) came into being under Babangida Administration, with the same old story to develop the Niger Delta. It was allegedly programmed to fail right from the beginning for many reasons including poor funding and hijack of contracts by many Abuja loyalists, most of whom came from outside the Niger Delta. A parallel body the Petroleum Trust Fund (PTF) was set up (which was a good thing) to develop the non-oil producing areas of the country. This PTF was well-funded to carry out road construction outside the Niger Delta.

The Niger Delta Development Commission (NDDC) was established in the year 2000 during the Obasanjo Administration to replace OMPADEC. Why the replacement? Why change of names? What was wrong with OMPADEC? Nothing. The poor funding suffered by OMPADEC was also extended to NDDC. Did the change of names to NDDC improve the funding of NDDC? The answer is NO.

To legitimize the monumental injustice in the Niger Delta. The following Acts were passed:
*   The Petroleum Act of 1967
*   The NNPC Act of 1977
*   The Land Use Act of 1978
The end game of all these Acts is that the people who own the land get peanuts while the Federal Government collects all the rents, royalties and petroleum profit taxes. The resultant effects are poverty, pollution of the environment, diseases and deaths, illiteracy and unemployment. So then, oil that should have been God's blessing is now turned to curse and deaths. Communities, out of folly, fight each other just because of a drop of oil, whereas those who cart away Billions of barrels of crude oil daily smile to their

banks in friendly countries!

You also begin to wonder whether oil is the only resource we have in Nigeria. The wealth from **solid minerals** is undoubtedly more than that from oil. The solid minerals are all deposited outside the Niger Delta. The laws guiding the exploitation of solid minerals are tailored to allow individual and States concerned to have free hand unlike the Petroleum and NNPC Act. Are we operating in the same country?

The writer has gone this far to show that it is unlikely that the "leopard will change its spots". Let us watch and see if they will subsequently and immediately take further right steps on the road map to eventual peace in the Niger Delta.

Let it be stated quite categorically that further talking shops will not help us at this stage. What is needed now is **ACTION**, after which we can continue with further dialogue. Why?

The reason is simple. The people have dialogued among themselves and come up with the following:-

➢ The Ogoni bill of Rights
➢ The Kaiama declaration
➢ Oron bill of Rights
➢ Egi declaration and Warri Accord

All these declarations are lodged in the offices of the Federal Government without any response.

Late Ken Saro Wiwa was a nonviolent man. Dialogue was his middle name. He popularised the slogan of self-determination.

Our elders and representatives from the Niger Delta were forced to walk out from the Constitutional Conference in Abuja because the hegemonic State did not want to hear any increase in the Derivation Fund to mere 25%, not to talk of 50%.

If it is dialogue the Federal Government wanted to solve the Niger

Delta crisis, PRONACO offered a peaceful way and means to resolve the crisis, which Alhaji Asari Dokubo also subscribed to. Any show?

Talking of the resolution of the Niger Delta crisis, the Federal Government set up its own committee in November 8, 2001 headed by Lt. General Alexander Ogomudia. It was set up to find ways of tackling the restiveness and also to bring lasting peace to the region. Its report was submitted to former President Obasanjo on February 19, 2002. The recommendations favoured the people of the Niger Delta hence the report was swept under the carpet.

So any further talks without ACTION will not yield anything. So what are the further <u>RIGHT STEPS</u> the duo of President Yar'adua and Goodluck Jonathan are to take to reach the promised land in peace and harmony, without fear of restiveness, hostage taking and blowing up of oil pipelines and installations?

Here are the further <u>RIGHT STEPS</u>:

*	Immediately repeal the obnoxious Acts and decrees vis-à-vis:

	The Petroleum act of 1969

	The NNPC Act of 1977

	The Land Use Act of 1978

*	Immediately approve 50% Derivation Principle as it was before the Nigerian Civil War.

*	Immediately pass a bill to restructure the country along True Fiscal Federalism

*	Urgent steps to massively develop the Niger Delta just as Abuja is developed, without going through any agency like NDDC. Abuja's development did not come through any agency. Direct allocation of funds from the Federal Government was (and is) the method for Abuja's

development. Use the same method to develop the Niger Delta. Link up the major communities producing oil. Construct modern roads as in Abuja. Link the communities with electricity PHCN grid, potable water, schools and universities. Provide jobs and infrastructural development.

*   Immediately release former Governor Alamieyeseigha on bail.

*   The 13% Derivation (which should be increased to 50%) should be lodged in a special bank account in trust for the Niger Deltans. Only the excess profit from the deposit should be expended on behalf of the people and in accordance with projects the people themselves choose. **<u>This 13% Derivation should not be given to any State administrator or Governor to use for any reason</u>**.

*   Pay reparation to communities like Oloibiri, Ogoni, Odi and others who have suffered considerable environmental degradation and despoliation.

*   Give Amnesty to the 'freedom fighters' and resettle them by employing them in the oil companies.

*   Immediately revert the decision of sale of oil refineries to private individuals. If the oil refineries in the Niger Delta must be sold, then sell to core Niger Delta State Governments or individuals or group of individuals in the Niger Delta, for instance Moni Pulo Oil Company.

Peace and harmony will immediately return to the Niger Delta and indeed Nigeria as a whole if the Government of President Yar'adua can be bold enough, sincere enough and willing to do justice.

If the above right steps are taken, President Yar'adua and Goodluck Jonathan would be writing their names in gold.

Let us do <u>justice</u> and make <u>peace</u> now before it is too late.

Comments

The relative peace we enjoy currently in the Niger Delta, was masterminded by Late President Yar'adua. Efforts should be made to honour all agreements. But the permanent solution to the Niger Delta issue is restructuring of the polity.

HOW TO FIGHT CORRUPTION IN NIGERIA

PUBLISHED BY THE HARD TRUTH, 2007

Corruption has become so synonymous with the name Nigeria that one is beginning to forget how many times our country Nigeria has been declared one of the most corrupt countries in the world by Transparency International. Corruption has been the bane of our socio-economic progress. Though corruption has been with us since our independence, it became worse in the last eight years necessitating the setting up of anticorruption outfits like ICPC and EFCC.

ICPC was inaugurated on September 29, 2000 and EFCC was established by an Act of the National Assembly on December 12, 2002, by President Olusegun Obasanjo, GCFR.

The new political dispensation led by the servant-leader, President Umaru Yar'Adua, has started the anticorruption crusade on the right footing by righting some of the wrongs of the last regime. But when one juxtaposes the President's stance with what has been going on in the House of Representatives (referring to the alleged N628 Million House renovation scam), one wonders if the servant-leader will have many supporters to make a meaningful impact in the fight against corruption.

Nigeria in her 47th year of Independence cannot afford to continue with the cankerworm called corruption. We cannot and should not continue on this ignoble path of corruption, if we are to make any meaningful and positive impact on the socio-political and economic development of our dear Nation and her people.

We have for too long "sidon looked" and in most times gleefully participated in the "come and chop" bazaar, making all of us guilty of our actions and inactions. As Professor Wole Soyinka said; "the man dies in all who keep silent in the face of tyranny", corruption is not only an injustice to our country and our compatriots but also an injustice to our psyche.

I therefore present this precious gift to our country Nigeria: **How to fight corruption in Nigeria.** I sincerely hope that this piece of writing will touch our hearts and assist us in the alchemical transformation we all need on the path of rectitude.

Below are some of the recommended ways and methods to fight corruption in Nigeria:

<u>POLITICAL RESTRUCTURING</u>

The foundational blocks on which Nigeria stands are soaked in corruption, and this corruption is permeating to all other segments within the country. As they say, "when the head of the fish is rotten the fish is gone". There is, therefore, need to restructure the country along True Federalism. Nigeria should be divided into six to eight regions. Each region, being autonomous, takes care of its resources and pays agreed tax to Central Government. With this arrangement, no one will be allowed to plunder the "national cake" accruing to a region from the real sweat of the masses.

Corruption thrives unobtrusively because the oil revenue from the Niger Delta is free! Remove oil from the equation and replace it with Groundnuts from the North or Cocoa from the South-West or Palm Oil from the South-South or Coal from the South-East and what you get is a steep decline in corruption.

<u>DECENTRALIZATION OF POWER</u>

Centralization of power also contributes to the degree and magnitude of corruption because it allows so much money in the hands of very few individuals. The resultant effect is that everybody goes to Abuja, cap in hand, begging or soliciting for funds by any means possible. It is therefore very easy for those controlling the excess funds, if not guided by moral rectitude, dole out to friends and relations or siphon the funds by any means or routes possible, sometimes even when due process is followed!

Decentralizing the vortex of power will surely reduce the level of corruption in the country.

PRESIDENTIAL SYSTEM OF GOVERNMENT

The Presidential system we are running is not suitable for a country like Nigeria. The system itself is very wasteful and expensive to run. When you combine these with majority of the people who are greedy and rapacious, what you have is corruption quadrupled. A system of Government that will invite party loyalists to "come and eat", a system that appoints Minister for a particular portfolio and then add Minister for State 1, Minister for State 2, with their complete retinue of advisers, assistants and media men cannot be said or adjudged to be suitable for us.

A Parliamentary system of Government with fewer representatives is likely to reduce the level of corruption in the country. If this is not possible then we need to reduce the number of ministers, legislators and other political appointees by one-third. This idea should extend to the States as well.

THE ISSUE OF ETHNICITY

The fight against corruption is hampered by playing the ethnic card to defend the indefensible whenever any "big fish" is caught in the net. This should not be so if we are to make progress in our crusade against corruption. There should be no sacred cows.

EMPOWERING THE PEOPLE

It is no gainsaying that corruption thrives in the fertile ground of illiteracy, unemployment, very poor remuneration and extreme poverty. We tend to water the seed of corruption if we continue to widen the gap between the haves and the have-nots. We encourage corruption when we pay workers a minimum wage of N8,500 per month in this era of triple-digit inflation. We know full well that N8,500 cannot last three out of thirty days in the month in a family of three (husband, wife and a child).

Education is therefore paramount in the fight against corruption. We need to back this up with full employment of all employable youths with pay commensurate with what obtains overseas. Those who are not employed should have generous monthly allowances. Shelter too should be made available to all our citizens. Corruption will thrive less in an atmosphere of sufficiency.

OUR WARPED MINDSET

Our mindset also plays a role in perpetuating corruption in our society. Everyone wants to get rich fast without putting in an iota of hard work. This is even worsened by another corrupt mindset: "if you cannot beat them, join them". For how long can we continue like this? We need to change these wrong perceptions and embrace hard work.

FLAUNTING OF WEALTH FROM CORRUPT ENRICHMENT

Unfortunately, our society encourages corrupt enrichment by honouring corrupt officials with chieftaincy titles and leadership positions. Consequently, such fraudulently acquired wealth is flaunted just like a cascade system, they win adherents and supporters. It is therefore not easy to fish out and isolate those who have plundered our patrimony.

ABSENCE OF DETERRENCE

This is the main reason why corruption is multiplying in geometric proportions. Many looters go scot-free with their loots. There is no deterrence. In few cases, where there is a semblance of deterrence as in plea bargaining, it is just like slapping one on the wrist! Why on earth do we ask someone to refund a negligible percentage of his stolen wealth and just walk away? If so, let us fling open our prison doors and ask the inmates to walk home on refunding a percentage of whatever they thought they stole! By this act, we are effectively encouraging others who are on their seats to steal more and more, enough for them to later refund a negligible percentage of whatever they would determine they misappropriated. **WONDERFUL!**
Such situations in China would instantly attract unimaginable consequences. These extreme measures are not advocated in Nigeria but at least we can follow the Philippines' examples of proper investigations and prosecutions.

INDEPENDENT AUDITING

The services of independent and honest auditors are sine qua non in the fight against corruption. They can be sourced locally or internationally to periodically audit the accounts of NNPC or its various components, Federal and State accounts, the Legislature, Judiciary and all other areas needing accounting procedures.

ELECTING THE RIGHT PEOPLE

This is the crux of the matter. We need to elect the right people to take charge of our political and economic affairs. The moment we allow unworthy people, by act of cowardice, docility or bribery, to rig themselves into power, then we are willingly sowing the wind of corruption and must therefore be prepared to reap the whirlwind of underdevelopment and misery. That is why the INEC Chairman and the Commissioners should not be appointed or nominated by the President or political party in power. The INEC should be truly independent from the influence of the Executive, and fortified to exhibit its credibility and trustworthiness as an unbiased arbiter.

LEGISLATIVE POLICING

The legislature, apart from making laws for our country, has the capacity to carry out oversight functions. So, if the legislative Houses in the Federal and State governments are peopled by men and women of integrity and honesty, corruption will nosedive to all time low within the system

But what if the legislative bodies themselves are corrupt, who checks them? That is the million-dollar question. That is the reason why we must elect people with proven integrity and honest means of livelihood to the various Houses, if we are to make appreciable progress in our march towards Millennium Development Goals and our anticorruption crusades.

PERKS OF OFFICE AS INCENTIVES FOR CORRUPTION

One of the causes of corruption and violence in our electoral system is the attraction to the huge salaries and allowances attached to elective offices. The first thing newcomers do is to quickly hike their salaries and allowances, buy bulletproof and tinted SUVs and run to overseas countries for birthday parties and naming ceremonies.

It is also because of this that elections are always rigged and declared "do or die" with its attendant violence.

If we are to make any meaningful inroads in the fight against corruption, then no political figure should earn more than a professor, not even the President!

STRENGTHENING THE EFCC AND ICPC

The EFCC is doing a good job. They should be allowed to continue but with few modifications or adjustments. They should conform to the rule of law. The era of answering to the Presidency is gone for good and there should be no selective investigations and prosecutions. What is good for Peter should be good for Paul. Most importantly, the heads of EFCC and ICPC should not be appointed by the President, but by an independent body.

STRENGTHENING THE POLICE AND OTHER SECURITY AGENCIES

The corruption we see in the Police Force is just a mere reflection of what obtains in the society. They are poorly paid and poorly armed. If we increase their minimum wage from N10,000 or so per month to at least N50,000 as suggested by a past Governor, we will drastically reduce the level of corruption in the Force.

We can strengthen the police and other security agencies to fight corruption by providing adequate remunerations, improved conditions of service, adequate training, proper equipment and severing its political attachment to the Executive.

STRENGTHENING THE JUDICIARY

This is a very crucial aspect in the fight against corruption. If the entire judiciary is corrupt, the whole country is finished because most, if not all, looters can easily bribe their way out of prison or being shielded from mere investigations!

The judiciary has a very crucial role to play in elections as it is practised today. Rigging, manipulation of election results and extreme violence have since assumed frightening dimensions in our polity. We should therefore move away from this dangerous path because electoral corruption is the worst form of corruption, and the "grandmother of corruption". Men and women of integrity and honour should be allowed to continue to occupy such posts. Any corrupt judicial officer should not only be asked to quit but be prosecuted as well. That is why they are seen to be the last hope of the common man.

Comments

This article on corruption was written in 2007, and published by the Hard Truth. All the solutions I proffered are still very relevant today, if not more relevant.

In fact, my book titled "How to Fight Corruption in Nigeria" written in 2011, gives a broader perspective, and it is a must-read for every Nigerian.

Strengthening the Judiciary can be achieved by removing the influence of the Executive. The President shouldn't be the one to appoint or nominate the Chief Justice of Nigeria and other Judicial appointments. If this is allowed to continue, the Judiciary will always be subservient to the Executive arm of Government!

General consensus of opinions is that victory in elections should not be decided by the Judiciary. Actual winners of elections should come from the ballot box and not from the courts, as is practiced in India, Brazil, Indonesia and many other countries.

The commonsense here is that if the Judiciary is compromised (after all, they are humans), democracy is compromised.

This article reminds us of a popular comedian, John Okafor, Mr. Ibu, who in his song, "Annoyed Annoyed", in 2005, captured the scenario then compared with the present.

He sang:
"Nigeria dey shake O
Our country dey tumble
Africa dey shele
Everybody dey cry
Poor man dey suffer
Rich man dey cry
We get pump, water no dey run there
We get kerosene, poor man no dey buy am
We get fuel ten litres ten dollars
Some road for this country, motor no dey run there
If not for okada some people for don die o"

The main cause of mass poverty, gross underdevelopment and seeming helplessness pervading the Nigerian society is due to massive corruption.

That is why Nigeria that started almost evenly with the Asian Tigers like Malaysia, Singapore and South Korea, is down in the valley and the Asian Tigers are now on top of their world!

More than 99% of our oil wealth is in the hands of few individuals who siphon the money abroad to build five-star hotels, oil refineries, modern hospitals with state-of-the-art equipment, stadia, banks, choice property in all State capitals of the world. It has been stated that the sum of all the monies stashed away at home and abroad is more than the total assets of Britain and France combined!

In Qatar and other oil producing countries, every citizen is comfortable in his or her own house with all the good things of life, including well-paid jobs. The standard of education in such countries is comparable to those attainable in highly civilised lands. The healthcare delivery system is worthy of emulation. The roads are well maintained and kept neat at all times.

In Nigeria, the money that could have been used to offer services to humanity is taken out to develop the economies of other nations. The endgame is that we have very bad roads and we are among the poorest countries, even in Africa. Our education and health sectors are far from the best. That is why Transparency International has always labelled us low in their rankings.

<u>2014 NATIONAL CONFERENCE (NC): ISSUES AND THE WAY FORWARD</u>

This article was written and sent to the Nations Newspaper, October 8, 2013.

The deafening call for National Conference (NC) has been submerged for years. The sudden resurgence of the call is a welcome development, irrespective of the motive behind it. The need for the NC is overwhelming, considering the chaos in the country with its attendant insecurity. The NC is to address the imbalance in the country as well as the socio-political injustices that stare us in the face! What we have is a Constitution, largely put together by the military, which is incapable of righting the political wrongs.

Previous Conferences did not see the light of the day because of insincerity of our leaders and seeming opposition, from others. We made some progress in one of the previous Conferences but it did not see the light of the day because some zones were vehemently opposed to the NC. The fear is that the NC can lead to the disintegration of the country, and that the National Assembly is already in place to tackle or take care of the political issues bothering the minds of the various ethnic nationalities.

It is pertinent here to address such fears early in the discourse. They argue that sovereignty belongs to the people, and that this sovereignty has been handed over to the National Assembly and so it is their responsibility to act on our behalf.

Many others have argued that the National Assembly members were elected primarily to make laws according to the Constitution on ground. They further posit that they are not empowered by law to make a brand new Constitution. It is true, however, that they can amend parts of the Constitution, but not to make a new one.

What Nigeria needs is to make a new Constitution agreeable to all stakeholders of the country, and that will include all of us, not one suiting a section of the country, but detrimental to other sections or zones.

Some have also argued that the National Assembly, as presently constituted, is very faulty because some of them were selected and not elected. This school of thought argues strongly that the present skewed distribution of Representatives, mainly based on the spread of Local Government Areas (LGAs) in the various sections or zones of the country, is one of the injustices that should be addressed by the National Dialogue.

Now let me address the fear that the dialogue is likely to divide the country. This cannot be true! What will agitate the minds of the people is the refusal to allow the people to come together to fashion out what is agreeable to all sections or zones of the country. The refusal to right the socio-political maladies and wrongs inherent and embedded even in our present Constitution is what should be discussed. Every reasonable Nigerian wants to live in one united country. Nobody is itching to pull out of Nigeria. The propaganda that Nigeria will split is not true. The silent reason why those who are opposing the dialogue is because they don't want to let go the advantages they enjoy.

Many opponents of the NC have talked about leaving out contentious issues. Which issues are contentious?

People have also disagreed sharply on whether the conference should be sovereign or not. Whether sovereign or not, the decisions arrived at, at the conference should not be diluted or doctored by any individual or group of individuals, including National

Assembly members. The decisions reached should be implemented for the good and unity of the country. If need be, such decisions or resolutions can be referred to a referendum.

Some who oppose the NC are likely to tolerate it if there are "no go areas". Why should people talk of "no go areas"? Are we in slavery? Are we not free to discuss matters militating against our survival, if I may ask? There should be no restrictions on what to discuss. The fear that the country will disappear if such is allowed is completely unfounded and misplaced.

Mr. Anthony Sani, the spokesman of the Arewa Consultative Forum (ACF) in his recent interview with Sunday Punch of 6th October,2013 stated: "the North does not believe the problems of this country have to do with the structure, form of government and the laws. The problems of this country are as a result of collapse of national ideals, collapse in moral values…"

This could be true! But the problems of Nigeria take root from this faulty structure of the Nigerian foundation, which has given rise to the said collapse of national ideals, moral values and conscience.

This faulty foundation has given rise to political corruption, which has given birth to twins; a failing state and insecurity as occasioned by kidnapping, armed robbery, banditry and killings.

Few examples of political corruption will suffice:

- Running a Federal System of Government on paper but unitary in practice, whereby every State Governor runs to Abuja, cap in hand, to share oil money coming from the environmentally devastated Niger Delta.
- Skewed distribution of States and LGAs in the country
- Skewed distribution of resources
- Rigging of election results

What are the issues that must be addressed amicably?

1.   **FEDERAL OR UNITARY SYSTEM?**

What we are practising is solely a unitary system. This should be abolished in favour of Federal System. The country could be divided into 12 zones or regions: 6 in the North and 6 in the South. The 36-State structure should be subsumed within the regions. Each region should be free to man its resources and pay 50% tax to the Federal Government. This will rekindle positive competitive spirit and lead to real development as seen in the First Republic.

The system of Government we are running with 36- state structure plus the Federal Capital Territory with Governors and retinue of Commissioners, Assistants, and multitude of members in all the State Houses of Assembly, coupled with 774 LGAs with equal number of Chairmen and all the Supervising Councillors, is not only wasteful but cannot be sustained for long in a oil-dependent economy soaked in corruption.

The solution to this problem is to restructure the country into twelve regions or zones (akin to twelve States creation by former Head of State, Yakubu Gowon) with a Central Government. This will reduce the profligacy to the barest minimum, thus releasing funds for capital projects.

2.   **CREATION OF LOCAL GOVERNMENT AREAS (LGAs)**

In a real Federal System, only two tiers of Government operate: the Federal Government and the Federating Units or States. LGAs have no place at all. Each region or zone as mentioned, will be free to create as many States and LGAs as feasible, and the States and LGAs so created will be funded by the regions or zones and not the Federal Government.

3. **BLOATED BUREAUCRACY**

Nigeria is failing because of the bloated bureaucracy and the monumental wastage in operation. Presidential system of Government is expensive and prone to corruption. Parliamentary system may be better?

In the Executive, we need to reduce the number of Ministers from 42 or so to a maximum of 20. There should not be duplication of Ministers as we are operating currently. The number of parastatals should be reduced drastically. Those having similar functions should be merged in keeping with Orosanye's Report.

The Legislature is also contributing to the bloated bureaucracy and profligacy. We have 109 Senators and 360 members of the House of Representatives, giving a total of 469. The bicameral legislature we are running should be replaced with a unicameral legislature, with a total number ranging from 100 to 200.

4. **HIGH COST OF GOVERNANCE**

Our politicians are alleged to be the highest paid in the world. Richard Dowden, the Director of Africa Royal Society in London, was invited as Guest Speaker on our 51st Independence Anniversary. In his address, he gave the annual take-home pay for Senators as 2 Million US Dollars. (1 Million as salary, 1Million in allowances). The above figures were corroborated by Prof Itsay Sagay, SAN, who gave a figure of 240 Million Naira for Senators (1.7 Million US Dollars) and 204 Million Naira annual take-home for Members of House of Representatives. The take-home packages for the President, Vice President, Ministers, Governors and Commissioners, Local Government

Chairmen etc are not known. This is not to talk of security votes that turn into Billions of Naira. The possibility of paying only allowances to politicians should be discussed and implemented. This will limit the political space for those who are going there not to serve the people but their pockets. It will sound reasonable if the President's allowance (not salary) is pegged at the maximum, not above the salary of a professor in the University system. Those below the President of course will have an equivalent of Senior Registrar etc.

5.   **CORRUPTION**

The principle of 'prevention is better than cure' should be applied here. Where this is not possible, proper investigations and diligent prosecutions should be the order of the day.

There shouldn't be sacred cows, and no plea bargaining should be entertained. Convicted persons should be asked to return all stolen money and property with interests!

6.   **FREE AND FAIR ELECTIONS**

Electing the right people free from rigging, violence and intimidation should be discussed. To achieve the above, the Electoral body should be truly independent in their appointments and funding. In fact, Justice Uwais Recommendations should be dusted and implemented fully.

7.   **SECTION 308 IMMUNITY CLAUSE**

This should be tabled in the Conference. Clear differentiation should be made between civil and criminal cases. Immunity should be allowed for civil cases only.

8.   **STRONG INSTITUTIONS**

As President Obama said during his visit to Ghana in 2009:

In the 21st century, capable, reliable and transparent institutions are the key to success — strong parliaments and honest police forces; independent judges and journalists; a vibrant private sector and civil society. Those are the things that give life to democracy, because that is what matters in people's lives.

We need strong and independent institutions such as Legislature, Judiciary, the Press, EFCC, ICPC etc.

If the above issues and many others are discussed in a brotherly spirit and sincerely implemented, one Nigeria of our dreams will be realised.

Nigeria is more likely to slide into disunity and chaos if we fail to right the wrongs of society.

HOW WILL THE DELEGATES FOR THE CONFAB BE APPOINTED, SELECTED OR ELECTED?

Opponents of this confab frown at the suggestion of inviting all ethnic nationalities. How, they argue, will it be fair to have a major ethnic nationality have equal representation with those from a minority group.

They have a point here, but we should remember that we are not going there to vote, but to have a general consensus on how best to achieve the greatest development for the greatest number of people under the prism of justice, unity and equity.

COMMENTS

The issues discussed in this article are very germane and still very much relevant to the resolution of the foundational problems plaguing and tearing the country apart.

As lovers of this country, we should rally round, bury our perceived personal, ethnic and religious differences and set in motion the implementation of the 2014 National Conference Resolutions. There is no other easy way out!

OPEN LETTER TO PRESIDENT–ELECT, MUHAMMADU BUHARI ON HOW TO FIGHT CORRUPTION IN NIGERIA.

BACK PAGE OF NEW TELEGRAPH, TUESDAY, MAY 26, 2015

Your Excellency,

I wish to join all well-meaning Nigerians to congratulate you on your success in the last general elections. I wish you a successful tenure.

I am emboldened to write this letter to you because of your good intentions of fighting corruption - the monster **Octopus** in Nigeria. You have stated quite correctly the right steps you would want to take to fight this monster: appointing men and women of integrity in your cabinet, reducing the bloated bureaucracy, initiating some probes etc, etc.

All the above and many more are outlined in the book I wrote in 2011, "HOW TO FIGHT CORRUPTION IN NIGERIA". Full details of the contents of the book can be read online www.amazon.com. Type Daminabo Sonny Briggs.

Sir, fighting corruption is not an easy job. Corruption can be taken as a giant octopus, with many malignant tentacles. Since killing corruption completely is not possible, killing the octopus is also not possible. But we can immobilise the octopus by cutting off many, if not all the tentacles.

Corruption has done incalculable damage to our society. It is the major obstacle to our growth and development. In fact, it is the root cause of the insecurity and violence we see now manifesting in the country. It destroys the socio-politico-economic environment and democracy. It robs us of creating wealth, and thus employment opportunities for our teeming and jobless graduates. It robs us of direct foreign investments, it robs us of opportunities that tourism can offer!

Corruption leads to drastic reduction in budgetary allocations to education, healthcare, energy and power, transport etc. with the attendant negative indices. Corruption breeds poverty, disease and death. Corruption devalues our Naira, which is plunging to all time low of one dollar to One Hundred and Eighty Two Naira (contrast this to one dollar to sixty six kobo in the 70's).

The negative effects of corruption cannot all be discussed here, but our country can be treated as a pariah State in the comity of Nations, and can even lead to economic collapse and disintegration.

The irony or paradox here is that all these are happening in a country that has been the sixth producer of crude oil over the decades. This is so because of corruption and noninvestment for future generations!

What is corruption, you may ask? Corruption is not only stealing of public funds, taking or giving bribes, kickbacks, embezzlement etc. It goes beyond all these. The fact that we profess to run a Federal System of Government, while in actual fact we practise a quasy-unitary system is, itself, corruption. The fact that we spend 70 to 80 percent of our annual budget on recurrent expenditure, leaving little or nothing for capital projects is corruption. The fact that few individuals, our leaders, earn Millions of Naira per month, while majority of the people are jobless, and workers live with N18,000.00 minimum wage is corruption in high places. The fact that we have skewed distribution of States and Local Government

Areas in the Federation is corruption multiplied.

All these are acts of Political Corruption we have not been able to address!

How are we fighting corruption or how do we want to fight corruption when the above mentioned acts of corruption are the main issues, and the crux of the corruption matter? Corruption cannot be fought successfully without resolution of the above issues.

Corruption can easily be divided into Political, Bureaucratic, Electoral Corruption, and others. Political Corruption is the mother of all corruption. And what is Political Corruption? This occurs when politicians and political decision-makers, who are entitled to formulate, establish and implement laws in the name and welfare of the people, are themselves corrupt.   It also occurs when policy formulation and legislation are tailored to benefit politicians, legislators and their cronies and ethnic enclaves.

The magnitude of corruption in Nigeria is so gargantuan that it is difficult to get the true picture. Our National Assembly came up with statistics some years ago that Nigeria loses about three Trillion Naira annually to corruption through the Federal Civil Service, States, and Local Governments.

Happily, Transparency International (TI) and other global watchdogs have come up consistently with statistics that cannot be contradicted.

Let us look at Nigeria's performances on the accompanying TI table, showing the Corruption Perceptions Index (CPI) scores, from 1996 to 2014.

CPI scores from 1996 to 2005 showed Nigeria as the most corrupt or second most corrupt or within the bottom ten most corrupt countries in the world.

Our CPI scores from 2006 to 2014 ranged from 22 to 27 out of

YEAR	CPI SCORE OUT OF 100	NIGERIA'S POSITION
1996	6.9	54 out of 54
1997	17.6	52 out of 52
1998	19	81 out of 85
1999	16	98 out of 99
2000	12	90 out of 90
2001	10	90 out of 91
2002	18	101 out of 102
2003	14	132 out of 133
2004	16	144 out of 145
2005	19	152 out of 159
2006	22	142 out of 163
2007	22	147 out of 179
2008	27	121 out of 180
2009	25	130 out of 180
2010	24	134 out of 178
2011	24	143 out of 183
2012	27	139 out of 176
2013	25	144 out of 177
2014	27	136 out of 174

maximum of 100. The maximum score of 27 out of 100 was recorded in the years 2008, 2012 and 2014.

The slight improvements, though promising, on the CPI scores in 2008, 2012 and 2014, were not statistically significant. However, it should be noted that countries having CPI scores less than 50 out of 100 have serious corruption problems. So Nigeria's maximum of 27 out of 100 shows that we are in the bottom group of most corrupt countries.

The gloomy picture from TI is replicated by other Reports from:

• **Global Competitiveness Index (GCI) 2010:** The World Economic Forum, ranked Nigeria 127th out of 133 countries, relying on criteria such as electricity supply, infrastructure deficit, accountability, macro-economy, health/education, technological readiness and business sophistication innovation.

In 2012, GCI ranked Nigeria 115th out of 144 countries.

• **The 2011 Human Development Index (HDI)** released by United Nations Development Program (UNDP) placed Nigeria 156th out of 187 countries. This ranking was based on education, income and life expectancy.

In 2012, HDI, placed Nigeria 153rd out of 187 countries.

In 2014 HDI ranked Nigeria 152nd out of 187 countries.

• **MO Ibrahim Index of African Governance** showcases Nigeria's gloomy picture more vividly amongst African countries. The index relies on four categories of governance: Safety and Rule of Law, Participation and Human Rights, Sustainable Economic Opportunity and Human Development.

In 2010, this survey ranked Nigeria 40th out of 53 African Countries.

In 2011, Nigeria was ranked 41st out of 53

In 2012, Nigeria was ranked 43rd out of 52

In 2013, Nigeria was ranked 41st out of 52

In 2014, Nigeria was ranked 37th out of 52 African countries.

It is important to look at the possible causes of corruption and know where to lay the blame:

- **Weak or Absent Traditional Moral Values**

This is due to defective upbringing of our children and wards. Here we are all guilty. Therefore, we should not point accusing fingers at Government functionaries. If we are to fight corruption from source, this is where we should direct all our efforts on changing the mindsets of our children and wards as they grow up.

We, as parents, should show good examples, and not to encourage our children to cheat in examinations, and, in fact, go all out to pay others to write such examinations for our children.

- **Greed**

This is a major cause of corruption. The get-rich-syndrome is embedded in many of us. We are obsessed with materialism, and always looking for dubious shortcuts to affluence, without hard work!

- **Will to Fight Corruption**

The will to fight corruption is not lacking but it is feeble, and it is not translated to the reduction of corruption in the society, thereby promoting impunity.

- **Attitude of condoning corruption**

This is one major impetus for the rising level of corruption in Nigeria. There is worrying trend of the glorification of ill-gotten wealth, as we enjoy sycophancy and giving chieftaincy titles and national awards to those perceived to be corrupt.

- **Extreme poverty, poor remuneration, disparity in salaries and allowances and unfairness in distribution of**

resources can all lead to corruption.

Unusually high and unjustifiable salaries and allowances allegedly paid to politicians and their appointees lead to high level of corruption, poverty and underdevelopment, do-or-die politics, politics of bitterness and violence.

Back to some other causes of corruption:

Oil and Gas

The discovery of oil is expected to be source of blessing to the citizens of Nigeria, especially to the people of the Niger Delta Region. But this has since turned to curse and tragedy. This is so because of non-investment for future generations, and because oil is seen or taken as free for all. The oil is a source of corruption. If we take away oil from the Nigerian space, corruption is likely to be reduced by 60-80 percent.

Oil is a tragedy because of pollution and eventual destruction of the Niger Delta environment, lives and property. Apart from this environmental devastation, the Niger Delta Region is under-developed. Oloibiri, where oil was first struck in commercial quantities in 1956, is a good example of abandonment after sucking out the oil in its bowels! This is the height of political corruption. Politicians and political parties should start from the Niger Delta and quickly develop the Niger Delta Region just as Abuja was developed from virgin forest to its present state. Repair and development of the Niger Delta Region should be the major concern of any occupant in Aso Rock. This is the way to right the political wrongs.

- **Lack of accountability and transparency**

Accountability and transparency are essential ingredients in the fight against corruption. Are we showing such character in our polity?

- **Non declaration of assets**

Declaration of assets is a major ingredient in the fight against corruption. How many of our political leaders declare their assets? If so, was it done in the open, for people to raise queries, if any?
Declaration of assets should rightly be done before, during and after the tenure of office.

- **Practice of unitary system**

The institutionalization of a system that is Federal in name but unitary in practice is one of the contributory causes of corruption. This concentrates power at the centre, and is bound to lead to infighting, corruption, desperation to be in charge of affairs and violence.

The corruption attendant in the desperation to attain power at the centre can be greatly reduced if we restructure the country along True Federalism, dividing the country into twelve geopolitical zones. Each zone sourcing its resources, and paying taxes to the centre. This is likely to usher in peace and stability. Unfortunately, we were unable to summon up the courage necessary to do the right things based on the 2014 National Conference Recommendations. It is even doubtful if some other positive recommendations will ever see the light of the Day! Anyway, there is need to keep hope alive!

Bloated bureaucracy

This is contributing to the high level of corruption in the system. We need to revisit it in order to block the wastages and corruption.

Absence of public expenditure tracking

The good old days of the auditors should be brought back. The institution of Audit should be made independent. The Audit should also incorporate Public Expenditure Tracking. This will entail specially trained Auditors to continuously track and monitor huge funds allocated for projects.

Culture of sharing and not saving

This encourages corruption, as we are enamoured with sharing the "oil proceeds" i.e sharing the national cake, without baking it!

How do we fight the corruption in Nigeria?

Let me put on record and drop a "bombshell" here. What the writer is going to say now will shock many, but this is the unvarnished truth!

The way we fight corruption in Nigeria is very faulty. But the fault is not coming from the President or Governors or any politician or political parties! Not even from the police, EFCC or ICPC or what have you! Even if we bring Angels from heaven to run the Nigerian State as presently constituted today, the problems of corruption will not abate, but keep multiplying. This is because the fault is not in individuals but in the system. The problem is systemic. There is need to sanitise the system, then everything will fall in place.

The architectural design of the Nigerian Foundation is faulty, and this is the crux of the matter! And until we are ready to tackle the structural defects, all our efforts to combat corruption and political imbalance in Nigeria will not yield fruitful results.

The politicians and political parties should direct their energies and campaigns to the following strategies of "cutting off" the malignant tentacles of the giant Octopus:

We need to change our mindsets on corruption, emphasizing industriousness and honesty, starting with our children and wards in our homes, schools, churches and mosques. Introduction of anticorruption studies in our schools' curriculum is essential.

Restructuring the country along True Federalism is a prerequisite to attaining peace, stability and reducing corruption to the barest minimum.

The advantages of restructuring are obvious, the infighting to take power will be greatly reduced; there will be greater and healthier competition among the zones or regions, with less profligacy. Oil as a source of corruption will be taken away from the equation, and more people will guard and defend the resources from their own domains!

We should insist on conducting free and fair elections without violence, implementing Justice Uwais Recommendations.

The campaign and desire to fight corruption should reflect on how the political parties and politicians are fighting electoral corruption in their various parties. Imposition of candidates and godfatherism, intimidation and violence, outright purchase of delegates etc. are all elements of preelection rigging. No party can fight corruption where the emergence of their candidates is soaked in corruption. Conducting free and fair elections is very important to eliminate undesirable elements from assuming power. If we sow the seed of rigging, we will reap the fruit of corruption, poverty, under-development and economic collapse.

•   We should insist on strong and independent **Institutions such as:-**

Judiciary
Legislature
INEC
EFCC/ICPC
Audit
Police etc

There is need to cut down on the level of bureaucracy.

•   **We should also insist on reducing cost of governance**

The number of Ministers can be reduced to twenty or so, compared to the present number of forty or more, with further duplications. Unicameral legislature will serve Nigeria better than the bicameral we are operating now. Elimination of ghost workers both in the public and private sectors should be pursued with vigour.

•   **Insist on amending Section 308 immunity clause**

The immunity clause covers the President and Vice President, the Governors and their Deputies. The idea behind this is to shield them from litigations that can serve as unnecessary distractions. But it also promotes element of corruption. Anticorruption crusaders are advocating total abolition of the Immunity Clause. The middle way is to allow immunity for civil cases only, and not for criminal cases.

•   **Assets declaration**

This is a necessity for all aspiring leaders. Those who want to fight corruption must come to equity with clean hands.

•   **Effective deterrence**

This is one of the important tools for fighting corruption. There shouldn't be sacred cows. All those found guilty should face the "music". The offence committed should be commensurate with the punishment.

• **Independent Judiciary**
The fight against corruption cannot succeed if the Judiciary is also corrupt. Corrupt judges should be flushed out and prosecuted, and those engaged in unnecessary injunctions or conflicting political judgements should be removed from the system, and prosecuted as well.

Comments
This article was published by New Telegraph, May 26, 2015 and addressed to Mr. President-Elect, Muhammadu Buhari. I congratulated him on his promises to fight corruption in Nigeria.
This article summarized all the important or relevant steps to be taken in the fight against corruption.
The open letter contained a table showing Corruption Perception Index (CPI) scores from Transparency International (TI) from 1996 to 2014.

The Transparency International CPI scores from 2015 to 2023 as

Year	CPI Score out of 100	Nigeria's Position
2015	26	146 out of 180
2016	28	136 out of 176
2017	27	148 out of 180
2018	27	144 out of 180
2019	26	146 out of 180
2020	25	149 out of 180
2021	24	154 out of 180
2022	24	150 out of 180
2023	25	145 out of 180

shown above, show quite clearly that corruption in the last four years (2019-2022) of President Muhammadu Buhari's tenure has worsened.

At the global stage in 2019, Nigeria's position slipped two places to 146 out of 180 countries from the 2018 position of 144. Nigeria was also adjudged to be the 4th most corrupt country in West Africa in 2019 by Transparency International.

It is noteworthy that CPI scores are not even needed to affirm or corroborate, indisputably, the rising incidence of corruption. We are all living witnesses to all the shades and shapes of corruption in Nigeria.

The 2021 and 2022 CPI scores of 24 out of 100, with rankings of 154 out of 180 and 150 out of 180 countries respectively, are our worst rankings since 2013 under Buhari regime!

The rating was based on lack of transparency, nepotism, lack of better anti-corruption legal framework, bribery and extortion by Nigeria Police.

The Federal Government has kicked vehemently against the

damning reports, saying that the TI got it all wrong.
However, Nigeria recorded insignificant improvement in 2023 CPI score of 25 out of 100.

Nigeria's CPI scores in the last nine years (2015-2023) have hovered between 24 and 28, with an average score of 25.7 out of 100.

STRATEGIES FOR REDUCTION OF HIGH COST OF GOVERNANCE IN ORDER TO HAVE MORE FUNDS FOR NATIONAL DEVELOPMENT
WRITTEN JUNE 24, 2015

It is pleasing to observe that many well-meaning Nigerians and civil society groups today are becoming uncomfortable with our unbridled profligacy and wastefulness; and are now showing desired interest in the agitation for cutting down on the high cost of governance.

It is pleasing to me because this is what I have always advocated in my books:

> *How to fight corruption in Nigeria (2011)*
> *The problem with Nigeria (2014)*
> *(see Amazon.com, type Daminabo Sonny Briggs)*

The high cost of governance in Nigeria is a child of political corruption. Political corruption is the mother of all corruption, and it is itself as a result of the faulty structure of the Nigerian foundation. A lasting solution to this problem is to restructure the country along True Federalism. There is urgent need to divide the Country into twelve (12) geopolitical zones, each zone being autonomous, manages its own resources, and pays appropriate taxes to the centre. This is the right step to take, for the good and progress of the nation. If for any reason this cannot be done at this point in time, the closest to it, and our best bet, is to implement the recommendations of the 2014 National Conference Report.

The unitary or quasi-unitary system of government we are currently running is contributing to the high cost of governance. How so? The connecting link is our oil. The oil is taken as no man's property and free source of money for many. Remove oil and gas from this troubling equation and revert back to the days of the First Republic, you will see that the high cost of governance will disappear immediately. Why? Because resources from our individual and collective sweats will never be allowed to be wasted in the sea of profligacy!

Let me proffer some other strategies to reduce the high cost of governance, starting with the Executive.

In the First Republic, the Federal Government was served by not more than thirteen Commissioners.

Today we have not only forty or so Ministers, but also Ministers of State (which are duplications), in addition to numerous Personal Advisers. Obviously, this contributes to high cost of governance, as the appointed Officers will also have array of Officers working under them. So the way to reduce the high cost of governance is to limit the number of appointed Ministers and others to a manageable level of not more than twenty. This number can be sourced from a cluster of States. The Constitutional requirement of at least one Minister from each of the thirty-six States, is not and should not be sacrosanct. This Constitution is made for man and not man for the Constitution! Of course, the Constitution can be amended in this regard.

This same strategy can be extended to the States and Local Government Councils. We don't need more than 10 Commissioners in each State, if we are serious in cutting down on the high cost of governance.

Allied to the above, is the need to eliminate all ghost workers, Federal, States and Local Governments, and also to fish out all workers with fake certificates, no matter the grade level.

Remuneration for our political leaders is one sore point we urgently need to reconsider. It is not enough for one good-spirited individual to say "I'm cutting down on my salary". As good as this may seem, it does not solve the problem. Nigerians want to know, in this digital age, how much exactly is the total package for the President, Vice-President, Senators and Members of House of Representatives, Ministers, Special Advisers, Governors, Deputy Governors, Commissioners, Members of State Houses of Assembly, Chairmen of Local Government Councils and Supervising Councillors.

It is not enough for anyone to say "I am cutting my salary by 50% or 60%". The salary is not the issue, but the totality of the allowances combined with the salary, is the issue.

If someone's salary is N2 Million per month and his total value of allowances per month is N18 Million, it means his total package is N20 Million. If this person cuts his salary by 50%, it means he will get N1 Million per month, but when the allowances are added to the salary, the total package amounts to N19 Million per month. Is this cut significant?

It is alleged that Nigerian politicians are the highest paid in the world.

The statistics given below was sourced from **dailypost.ng/2012/07/2:**

President Obama earns	-$400,000 per annum
Prime Minister or United Kingdom earns	-$226,627 per annum
French President earns	-$318,072 per annum
South African President	-$296,112 per annum
German Chancellor	-$296,112 per annum
President of Namibia	-$164,506 per annum
President of Angola	-$60,000 per annum
President of People's Republic of China	-$10,633 per annum

President of Nigeria   -N14,058,820

                                            (Excluding allowances
                                            provided by
                                            government)
US Lawmaker   -$15,080 per month
UK Lawmaker   -$8,686 per month

For Nigerian Senators
Basic Salary (BS) per month   -   N2,484,245.50

<u>NOW LET'S GO TO ALLOWANCES</u>

Hardship Allowance	-50% of Basic Salary	N1,242,122.70
Constituency Allowance	-200% of "	"N4,968,509.00
Furniture Allowance-	300% of "	"N7,452,756.50
Newspaper Allowance	-50% of "	"N1,242,122.70
Wardrobe Allowance-	25% of "	"N621,061.37
Recess Allowance-	10% of "	"N248,424.55
Accommodation Allowance	-200% of "	"N4,968,509.00
Utilities	-30% of "	"N828,081.83
Domestic Staff	-35% of "	"N1,863,184.12
Entertainment	-30% of "	"N828,081.83
Personal Assistant	-25% of "	"N621,061.37
Vehicle Maintenance Allowance	-75% of "	"N1,863,184.12
Leave Allowance	-10% of "	"N248,424.55
Motor Vehicle Allowance	-400% of "	"N9,936,982.00
Severance Gratuity (One off Payments)	-300% of "	"N7,425,736.50

When all these allowances are added to the salary, the take-home pay swells to high heavens. Please give me a calculator!

Note that the above does not include Estacodes, duty tours etc.

I think it is the monetization policy that makes the Lawmakers' take-home pay look ludicrous. Some of the benefits should be provided by the Government, and not paid for e.g allowances for accommodation, vehicle, furniture etc as it is done for President and the Vice President.

Even so, the percentages of the basic salary allotted to the various allowances are too high!

However, the salaries and allowances of our politicians have not been independently verified or confirmed, thus amounting to yet-unproved allegations.

The Revenue Mobilization Allocation and Fiscal Commission (RMAFC) is statutorily empowered to determine the remuneration appropriate for political office holders. The brief of the RMAFC is not to please the politicians to the detriment of Nigerian citizens, as seen from the unbelievable total package differentials between the politicians and civil servants. RMAFC should have the interest and welfare of the masses at heart in allocating huge total package for politicians. They should remember and consider that millions of Nigerians are jobless, the few who are working are on N18,000.00 minimum wage, and that most of the workers and pensioners have not been paid for months in the midst of economic downturn.

Therefore, RMAFC should aim at pegging remuneration of political office holders at the level of civil servants. The highest paid political office holder should be encouraged to earn not more than the highest grade level in the civil service. This strategy will allow only selfless leaders to govern us while eliminating those whose eyes are on the treasury for selfish reasons.

At this juncture, two important issues are relevant: the issues of security votes and severance benefits. Reducing the cost of governance cannot be isolated from the issues of security votes and severance benefits. Who determines the amount of security votes for our leaders? Is it the RMAFC too, or the State Houses of Assembly? Some form of transparency in the operation of the security votes is more likely to reduce the cost of governance.

Severance benefits should be tailored along the lines of senior civil servants.

I am quite happy that President Buhari is enthusiastic about cutting down on the cost of governance, such as reduction in the ministerial list including personal advisers, selling off some of the aircrafts etc, etc. These are very laudable promises. We look forward to their fulfillment.

The cost of governance can also be reduced greatly if we cut down on convoys and travels undertaken by politicians.

Proper planning and budgeting in an atmosphere of accountability and transparency are prerequisites for reduction of cost of governance. The winning strategy is to make sure that in every budgetary allocations, the recurrent expenditure is less than that of capital projects.

On the legislature, many are clamouring for unicameral legislature rather than the bicameral one we are operating. I also think this is very crucial if we are to significantly reduce the cost of governance. Quite recently, Senegal has just done that, converting from bicameral to unicameral legislature. This will reduce cost of governance as the combined 360 Members of House of Representatives and 109 Senators gulp considerable amount of our budgetary allocation. Even the reduction from N150 Billion to N120 Billion for the Lawmakers is not good enough. This is so when you consider how much each Lawmaker takes from our economy.

A unicameral legislature is quite appropriate. A total number of 150 to a maximum of 200 will be more than enough to do the work of the legislature.

Even at this, part-time legislature is very desirable, as we should aim at paying allowances equivalent to what senior civil servants take home.

<u>**Comments**</u>

This article was written in 2015. This was deliberately timed, from the beginning of President Buhari's first term of office, to advise Government of the various strategies to be adopted in cutting down on the high cost of governance.

Unfortunately the promises made to reduce cost of governance have not seen the light of the day. My patriotic advice is that concerted efforts should be made to reduce cost of governance, especially in the midst of economic recession.

All the strategies, listed in my article in 2015, are still very much applicable and doable.

One thing we should not do is to take loans and waste them on the altar of consumption, corruption and profligacy. The huge burden of payment of such loans and interest will be too much and unbearable on generations yet unborn!

CONSTITUTIONAL AMENDMENTS IN NIGERIA – MOVEMENT WITHOUT MOTION?

A lot of legislative energy has been put into the cauldron of Constitutional amendments. This current attempt on the 1999 Constitution is the fifth. But many have argued that the 1999 Constitution, we are operating is in fact Decree 24 of 1999, signed by the Military. The question is how can we amend a military decree?

It is pertinent here to explain how we came to this 1999 Constitution, brewed and served by the military. The military was not only clever in military tactics, but also very savvy in political sagacity. No one could or can blame the military for what they did.

As Shakespeare said: "The problem is not in our stars…".
The folly and greed of not only the politicians but also the Nigerian citizenry contributed to a very large extent the berthing of the 1999 Constitution.

How did we arrive here?
The clamour for democracy was on a high crescendo with the democratic forces' disapproval of continuous military rule. And when finally the promise of democracy was announced, the people were naïve to rush to embrace it without putting in place or negotiating the right Constitution that would drive the democracy. Some vocal and patriotic National Democratic Coalition (NADECO) Chieftains like late Chief Abraham Adesanya, Chief Ayo Adebanjo and others insisted on seeing the Constitution first before "jumping into the arena, blindfolded".

The voices of those championing this school of thought i.e. agreeing

on acceptable Constitution before democratic elections, were soon drowned in a cesspool of political naivety, ignorance and idiocy. However, the military insisted on elections first before Constitution. It is painfully concerning to compare the Nigerian situation with how the citizens of South Africa, especially the African National Congress (ANC), led by their iconic former President, Nelson Mandela, handled the idea of which would come first: acceptable Constitution before elections or elections before Constitution.
The ANC insisted that the Constitution which would define the type of structure the government would run must come first before the elections. The Constitution of South Africa was therefore, promulgated on December 10, 1996, and came into operation on February 4, 1997.

In our own case, it was unimaginable that we did not even take the South African example of insisting on the Constitution before elections. So the sad reality was that by the time former President Olusegun Obasanjo took office as the elected democratic President of Nigeria in 1999, no one, not even the President had set eyes on the Constitution that was to direct the democratic structures of the country!
Wonderful!

It is therefore not surprising why we are finding it very difficult to change the Constitution or amend it in such a way as to give the true picture or semblance of Federalism.
Let us now constructively examine the Fifth Amendment of our Constitution. I quite agree that Constitution amendment is not a tea party. I sympathise with the lawmakers for this arduous task, especially in a multilingual, multiethnic and multireligious country. The difficulty in reaching acceptable consensus on the best structure to move the nation forward is further compounded by ethnic and religious considerations, occasioned by lopsided representations in the House of Representatives.

In spite of all challenging problems, the National Assembly should be given some kudos for a number of positive developments. Such positive developments include:
✓   Rejection of pensions for Presiding Officers of the National Assembly. However, there is need to look and do something for exorbitant pensions for other arms of government.
✓   Rejection of the conferment of immunity on Presiding Officers of the   Legislature and the Judiciary.
        Here, further consideration ought to be given to amend section 308 Immunity Clause. It has been suggested that immunity should only cover civil cases and not criminal cases.
✓   Approval of independent candidacy
✓   Separation of Attorney-General's office from the Ministry of Justice
✓   Approval of State of Address
✓   Approval of financial autonomy for local Governments (LGs)
In spite of some of these positive developments, Prof. Itse Sagay, Femi Falana and many others believed that they were merely cosmetic because they did not address the "many elephants in the room" i.e. restructuring, security, economy etc.

Taking out some of the items from the Exclusive List to the Concurrent List without touching section 43 of the Constitution, where the Federal Government (FG) controls the lion share, and the States go cap in hand doesn't help matters, it worsens everything.
There are many "loud areas" where the National Assembly kept mute. There was no provision to address the immediate problems of Nigeria, such as restructuring, security of the nation and the economy. The culture of impunity was not addressed, without which we cannot make progress.

ON RESTRUCTURING.

The items covered by the amendments are totally irrelevant to our existential needs. According to Prof. Itse Sagay, what is most important to the country is restructuring (True Federalism). They did not talk about it. They kept silent on funding formula for the Federation and other tiers of Government. They ought to retain the 1963 Constitution under which each region retained 50% of their resources, gave 20% to the Federation and kept 30% as redistributable pool. The poorest States got more from the pool, while the rich States also got some. Why can't the National Assembly put or impute this laudable aspects in the Constitution for the smooth running and peaceful coexistence of the nation?

ON FINANCIAL AUTONOMY FOR LOCAL GOVERNMENTS

This seems to be a positive and acceptable decision to most people. However, we are easily carried away or enthused by financial autonomy. But what is financial autonomy without political autonomy? Political autonomy is more crucial than financial autonomy. We should not forget that local government is a State matter. It has nothing to do with Federal Government in a Federal setting. According to Prof. Itse Sagay, creating special accounts for LGs is not only irrelevant, it is also a surreptitious way of stamping constitutional authority on creation and distribution of LGs in the country.

There has been groundswell of oppositions to the unfair distribution of LGs in the country. This is the area National Assembly should address before talking of financial autonomy. The LGs should not be in the Constitution. In a Federal set up, such as ours, only two tiers are recognised – the Federal and States (which are the federating units).

The States are to determine how many local governments they want.

The Federal government has no business with LGs. Funding of LGs is for States, the States have to create budgets for LGs so created.

ON ISSUE OF STATE POLICE
The National Assembly was categorical on the issue of State Police, and that is that they are opposed to state police, a reminder of what the President, Mohammed Buhari, said on National Television that he is opposed to State Police.

The level of insecurity in the country cannot be addressed with the same hackneyed methods and policies we have been applying for decades on end. We need to think out of the box and look for smart policies to face current challenges. Therefore, State Police (and even Community Police) is the way to go.

Come to think of it, how can they say that they are opposed to the State Police when we have it already operating in the form of:
Hisbah in Kano
Amotekun in the West
Ebubeagu in the East

Concluding from what Femi Falana said, "We need to change our Constitution, not amend it". No matter the number of amendments, cosmetic or not, no significant progress can be made in the polity.

It is advisable that we go back to the Constitutional Conference Report of 2014. Even if we don't want to implement all, let us take salient resolutions and put them in our Constitution.

At this stage, nothing is cast in stones, all amendments will still go to the States and only 2/3 votes from 24 out of 36 States Houses' of Assembly will pass such amendments.

BORROWING INTO THE ABYSS

Borrowing is an act of receiving a certain amount of money with the intention that the receiver will have to return the same amount with or without interest, after a fixed span of time.

The money borrowed can be used for diverse purposes such as financing deficit budgets, various capital projects and other investments.

Most countries borrow to survive the harsh realities of existence. Nigeria's case is not an exception. Borrowing didn't start with the Government of President Buhari as shown below from Premium Times:

Former President Obasanjo met 28Billion Dollars as foreign debt in 1999.

Nigeria external loan by December, 2020, five years of President Buhari, was 28.57 Billion Dollars, giving an extra 21.27 Billion Dollars accumulated under Buhari's administration.

This approximates to three times the combined amount by past governments since 1999 (source:https://www.premiumtimesng.com).

The Debt Management Office (DMO) in its earlier report gave Nigeria's total debt as of December 31, 2015 as N 12.6 Trillion, and by December 31, 2021, our total debt has risen to N 39.56 Trillion.

I quite sympathise with the Government and the Finance Minister, Zainab Ahmed, in these trying times with a potpourri of challenges: covid-19 pandemic, the fall of the Naira, insecurity with its financial implications and recessions among others.

It was difficult not to borrow!

Let it be stated at the outset that there is nothing wrong in borrowing. The Finance Minister has stated clearly that the Government's borrowing is still within healthy and sustainable limits. Moreover, she admitted that "our expenditure especially staff emoluments have been increasing at a very fast rate, making it difficult to cope with funding. The idea is to borrow more money to meet demanding needs and all critical projects".

The administration has consistently argued quite convincingly that they are borrowing for infrastructure.

It is alright if it is so. But the nagging question is: can the infrastructure pay back the loans?

This question is relevant when you put into consideration the recent devastating train attacks!

The Finance Minister made the right diagnosis and suggested the right treatment, "so what we have to do is a combination of cutting down costs as well as increasing revenue".

She is quite correct, but are they cutting down costs and increasing revenue?

The realities on ground do not support her assertion if we are taking loans for local roads and schools. Who is going to pay, the premium times asked?   These are projects that should be funded from internally-generated revenue. Similarly, rail construction within the confines of Nigeria, and even to Niger, a neighbouring country, is not yielding or generating commensurate funds for repayment.

The Economist, criticizing the incessant borrowings and the huge amounts, feels "the borrowings are to cater for a lot of failures or to keep some activities going" saying, "how the loans are going to be paid is not in question for them and that's very unfortunate".

In the opinion of the Economist, we should take loans only for projects that have the ability to pay back.

If a project is not generating cash flow, it shouldn't be taken.

Now how many of the projects for which the loans were taken are generating enough money to pay back?

Further borrowings included 5.012 Trillion Naira to finance Government's budget deficit in 2022. The Nation's public debt burden increased further to 44.5 Trillion Naira as at November 11, 2021 as Senate approved 16.23 Billion Dollars and 1.02 Billion Euros loans requested by the President (source: https://www.vanguardngr.com)

The Finance Minister hinted that the Government would borrow to fund subsidy. This is ridiculous. How can we borrow to fund subsidy? This is borrowing to fund consumption. In the view of former Governor, Peter Obi, "what we pay for subsidy is payment for inefficiency, cost of demurrage at the ports and corruption".

According to Peter Obi, "our past and continued mismanagements of borrowed funds and borrowing for consumption are the major contributors to the monumental economic challenges confronting Nigeria today. If the borrowed funds were invested in critical areas of development, education, health and poverty alleviation, Nigeria would have developed far beyond what it is today".

In Prof. Pat Utomi's view, borrowing is not a bad idea. He said, "Nigeria cannot grow unless we invest. If borrowings can result to diversification, then it is good to borrow. But what we are frowning at is borrowing to meet our problems".

The crux of the matter is that borrowing for consumption or subsidy will lead us to economic abyss.

Many have argued quite correctly in the writer's view, that if we manage our resources prudently, there will be no need to borrow a kobo, rather we will lend to poverty-stricken countries! This is possible if we implement the time-honoured saying that we "cut our coat according to our cloth and not our size."

Between 1999 and September, 2017, Nigeria made 77 Trillion Naira from oil revenue (https://wwwranguardngr.com.ng).

What did we do with this humongous sums of money? Are there anything substantial on ground to show for this amount? This is profligacy and wastefulness which are painful ingredients of our "fantastic corruption"!

Even in these trying times, Nigeria is currently producing about 1.7 Million barrels of crude oil per day. Each barrel sells at about 100 Dollars per barrel (courtesy, Ukraine – Russia Crisis). Simple multiplication gives us 170 Million Dollars every single day. Why can't we utilize such revenues to take care of all our problems, infrastructures and save enough for future generations and in fact give loans to other needy countries? With all the money at our disposal, do we still need to borrow or even to borrow more money?

It is difficult to fathom the reason behind the predilection for incessant and huge borrowings. Is there anything secret or sinister we don't know?

Nigeria is getting poorer because the Government is borrowing for the wrong reasons? With this spate of borrowings, we are borrowing and digging into the abyss. Our generations yet unborn, even our great, great grandchildren will not be able to pay back the accumulated interests and principals.

Repayment of the loans decades ahead would be extremely difficult when currently we are spending ninety percent (90%) of our revenue in servicing debts. This is so because the borrowed funds are allegedly mismanaged and have not been properly and prudently invested.

World-class economists have frowned and warned us of the dangers in such borrowings, which are capable of leading us to economic ruins and collapse.

It is no-brainer to say that a country that goes "a-borrowing goes a-sorrowing". Nobody is opposed to borrowings if such are geared or directed to profitable ventures i.e. oil refineries or even modular refineries, investing on productive narratives and diversification of the economy to achieve economic prosperity.

Why on earth you ask, have we not built new refineries since 1999? The humongous sums of the money sunk into maintaining our old refineries have not yielded any modicum of maintenance. Why is it that the Niger Delta States are unable to build at least one modular refinery in each of the nine States of the Niger Delta?

Nigeria is blessed with human and material resources. Whatever the situation in Nigeria, oil exploration has not stopped. We have been producing crude oil locally and selling with huge profits as of today due to Ukraine – Russia crisis. As I have calculated in this piece, we are making over one hundred and seventy Million Dollars on daily basis. There is no reason or there are no reasons why such a country should be broke and going caps in hand for loans.

The loans we got from China may be problematic if and when we are unable to meet our obligations.

The main reason why we are in this mess is because of corruption. Fantastic corruption! It is the same corruption that is responsible for our inability to fulfill agreements with University lecturers (ASUU) and other associations. We waste so much money on frivolities and bureaucratic nonentities, leaving relevant and priority areas to suffer. We borrow money to sustain our extravagant lifestyles. We borrow money to build railways from Kano to Maradi in another country, but not from Port Harcourt to Lagos or Maiduguri! How much have we realised from the railways to repay the loans?

Permit me here to proffer solutions to our challenges and problems of borrowing or not borrowing. There are two major groups of actions we should (or better still must) take to bring us out from the abyss of continuous borrowings. The first group of actions should be geared towards cutting costs of governance, and thereby saving money. The second group of actions should be geared towards decent and acceptable means of increasing revenues. Therefore, combination of cutting costs of governance, saving money, increasing revenues with prudent and transparent management is the magic bullet or panacea for our borrowing woes.

Let us now consider in detail the first group of actions i.e. cutting costs and saving money:

❖   **Inevitability of restructuring**
The 36-State structure with 774 Local Government Areas (LGAs) is very expensive and wasteful. Billions of Naira can be saved if we opt for parliamentary form of governance. Even if we want to continue with the current Presidential system, we can reduce the federating units, zones or States to a maximum of 20 or 24; for the sake of equity, 10 or 12 in the North and 10 or 12 in the South. The federating units are to create LGAs and cater for them.

❖   We can also reduce the cost of governance by implementing Orosanye's Report of merging Ministries, Parastatals. We can also go further by jettisoning the idea of duplicating the offices and ministries - substantial Ministers and Ministers of State.

❖   We can cut down the cost of Governance by reducing the bloated bureaucracy. The number of Ministers and Commissioners at the Federal and States should be reduced to half or one-third of the present number.

❖   We can save Billions of Naira if we are all patriotic, by reducing the total pay package of politicians and politically exposed persons, especially the allowances. RMAFC should be mandated to carry out comprehensive downward review.

❖   Financial accountability and prudent management of funds and budgetary allocations are necessary. Independent Auditor General is a sine qua non for effective monitoring of funds and applying modern money-tracking methods. The activities of Bureau of Public Procurement should be strengthened.

❖	Stoppage of huge pensions and severance packages to politically exposed persons is long overdue. If pensions should be paid to such Officers it shouldn't be more than what obtains in the Civil or Public service. The idea of owning residential buildings in the State capitals and Federal capital should be jettisoned.

❖	Same thing should be applied to security votes. Every avenue for wasteful spending should be blocked: large entourage for oversea trips, use of expensive cars, use of fleet of aircrafts, budgeting for cutleries annually [good quality cutleries do not rust].
The presidential aircrafts should be reduced to save cost of maintenance.
Incessant and unnecessary travels should be stopped.
The crave for owing private jets should be looked into.
We will save Billions, if not Trillions, of Naira if we truly fight corruption.

Corruption should be fought without bias or hatred, those found guilty by reason of law should be made to refund the loot with interest! The idea of plea bargaining promotes corruption. It should not be allowed because someone who embezzles Ten Billion Naira can decide to bring out Ten Million Naira only as part of the bargain and pocket the rest! Looted funds so recovered should not be stolen or shared among so-called whistle blowers! No sacred cows should be entertained.

The second plank of bailing ourselves out from the borrowing abyss is considering the second group of actions. There are multiple areas where Nigeria can make Trillions of Naira if we put our acts right without the need to borrow, such areas include, but not limited to:

❖	Modular Refineries, which are simplified refineries requiring significantly less capital investment and can be set up in most of the

Local Government Areas especially in the Niger Delta States. This will not only generate needed funds and take care of unemployment issues but also eliminate the menace of the vexatious and deadly soot threatening the lives of the people in the Niger Delta …

❖   Investing in education, health, modern Agriculture, Technological innovations and entrepreneurship.

❖   Investing in Arts/Culture, tourism and sea transportation.

❖   Massive rehabilitation of roads /bridges /rails with a view to introducing low and fair tolls. This will eventually cover the cost of infrastructure and yield profits with prudent and transparent management.

Six quick examples in Niger Delta:
- Construction of Roads/Bridges connecting Port Harcourt, Bakana, Isaka, Tombia, Bukuma and Buguma

- Construction of PH/Bonny Roads/Bridges.

- Construction of Borokiri/Okrika Bridges

- Construction of Roads/Bridges connecting Kula, Idama and adjoining communities to Degema.

- Construction of Ikukiri/Tombia Bridge

- Construction of a single bridge connecting Agada in Abua Local Government Area to Degema.

❖   Investing in Information and communication Technology with its inherent economic gains.

❖   Investing in Artificial Intelligence generated-gadgets

❖   Massive investment in Sports can yield enormous amount of funds. A good example is the Premier League in the United Kingdom.
Sporting activities like Football, Athletics, Wrestling, especially our traditional Wrestling, Boxing, Lawn Tennis, and Chess and many others can all assume the status of money-spinners.

❖   Investing in manufacturing of drugs and vaccines from local herbs and indigenous engineering.
Nigeria can borrow if such funds are geared towards profitable ventures.

In summary, Nigeria doesn't need to borrow if our God-given enormous resources are prudently and transparently managed. We can achieve this by cutting down, to the barest minimum, the cost of governance, reducing and eliminating profligacy, wasteful spending, corruption and increasing sources of revenue generation.

HOW TO ELIMINATE RIGGING / ELECTORAL MANIPULATION OF RESULTS / SELLING AND BUYING OF VOTES IN THE NIGERIAN ELECTORAL SYSTEM.

Presidential elections and other elections holding in other climes are largely a beauty to watch:
- ✓ Campaigns without bitterness and violence.
- ✓ Nobody is shot before, during and after elections.
- ✓ No rigging, no manipulation of results
- ✓ No glitches
- ✓ No selling or buying of votes
- ✓ No appointed or selected candidates
- ✓ No godfatherism or godmotherism
- ✓ No militarization of election processes
- ✓ No shutting down of the activities of the country because of elections
- ✓ Results are out immediately
- ✓ Losers congratulate winners
- ✓ Nobody goes to tribunals/courts (with very few exceptions).
- ✓ No conflicting court judgements.
- ✓ And everybody is happy.
- ✓ And you have peace everywhere

Why is Nigeria's situation different and violent? This is sordidness on our part, the leaders, the politicians and the rest of us!

The writer will spare no effort or leave no stone unturned in presenting to the public, especially our legislators, the basic truths and facts distilled from many decades of research and meditation on the various impediments to peaceful, credible elections, free from manipulations and violence.

Corruption or fantastic corruption is the major impediment to the free, fair, credible and peaceful elections in Nigeria. There are different shades of corruption, some of which are very malignant. Here, in Nigeria, we pay much attention and emphasis on bureaucratic corruption, which is the kind of corruption the citizens encounter daily at places like hospitals, schools, police, custom, local licensing offices etc. But we neglect the more dangerous aspects of corruption, such as political and electoral corruption, which have the potentiality of bringing the whole Country into disrepute, anarchy or disintegration. Nepotism, cronyism and favouritism are all forms of political corruption, and in their extremes are capable of doing maximum damage to the fabric that holds us together. Rigging of elections, manipulation of results and other forms of electoral corruption can present itself in three categories: preelection, during election and postelection.

Preelection forms can masquerade as disenfranchisement of people by not registering them or registering a less significant number or making registration itself a cumbersome process, thereby making them lose interest. And when eventually they are registered, the permanent Voters Card (PVC) may not be available for voting for myriad of reasons! Special form of rigging revolves round alleged manipulated census figures. The population of some areas or communities can be overestimated or underestimated. This will undoubtedly give unmerited advantages or disadvantages to such communities.

A dangerous dimension of this category is the constant attack of some groups of people by alleged unknown entities. There are simple ways to arrest these anomalies. First, we should seek for reliable electronic device that is capable of capturing biometrics/registration and delivering PVCs to registrants at once.

The idea of registering and waiting for four to six months before getting PVCs is not in keeping with modern realities. Moreover, many will not be able to trace their PVCs they so laboured for!

Second, we need accurate data for our elections, and such data can only come from accurate census results.

Third, our security forces should be commended for their patriotic duties. They are urged to do more in apprehending the unknown perpetrators of evil.
Electoral corruption during elections is well-known to everybody, and the subject is well-ventilated in this discourse.
Just like corruption is widespread, rigging of elections and manipulation of results are allegedly not limited to any political party. It is said that almost all political parties get involved. The difference is the magnitude of involvement, those with "big chests dollarize the show".

Nigerians cannot continue to swim in the pool of electoral violence, rigging and manipulation of results ad infinitum, elections after elections. We need to think out of the box for the sake of honesty, truthfulness, justice, unity, fairness and transparency. How do we transmute our mindsets, attitudes, character and behaviour and conduct a resemblance of free and fair elections obtainable in civilized climes? Some beneficial ideas have been presented already, but here are more!

We as parents have failed in our duties and responsibilities of bringing our children and wards on the right moral path. As such, the children and wards are left on their own, abusing drugs and offering themselves as ready and willing pool of thugs for election rigging and other vices. We have also failed (out of poverty and ignorance) to offer them requisite and basic education. Since we have offered them nothing, they don't have anything to offer to society, other than acts capable of bringing down the Nation.

The remedy for this is offering compulsory free education to our youths and finding for them some form of gainful employment. This will drastically reduce the growing population of ready and willing participants for all forms of electoral violence.

Greed is another contributor to electoral violence. In the absence of job opportunities, many people take politics as the surest way to make "quick" money. Many subscribe to the Shakespearean quote, "Fair is foul and foul is fair". With this mindset, we resort to all manners of violence and manipulation of results, never minding if such drastic and ungodly actions lead to elimination of opponents.

On a very serious note, we can eliminate rigging and associated electoral malfeasance if we consider seriously the faulty structure of Nigeria and the Constitution, and be courageous enough to carry out restructuring of the polity. The do-or-die mentality or desperation to grab the Presidency will disappear when we restructure the polity. The Presidency will then have to contend mainly with Exclusive Legislative List, such as Security, Currency and International Relations.

Another contributory factor in electoral corruption is the humongous allowances attached to politically exposed persons. The mouth-watering allowances are great incentives to the institutionalization of violence.

But the problem is not with the politicians. There is a body responsible for allocating wages, and that body is the Revenue Mobilization Allocation and Fiscal Commission (RMAFC). It has been allegedly reported that Nigerian politicians are the highest paid in the world. So the "ball is in the court" of the Commission to do what is right. If the right thing is not done, it will ultimately drain our hard-earned and dwindling resources, needed for infrastructural development and welfare of the people. That is why many "thinking" people recommend Parliamentary to the Presidential system. The system we are running is too expensive and not sustainable in the long run with Federal Government, 36 States plus Federal Capital Territory and 774 Local Governments to contend with!

Another sore point in our management of electoral systems, which invariably can lead to some form of rigging and other vices, is the appointment of INEC Chairman and Commissioners by the President. At the States' level, the Governors also appoint their own Chairmen and Commissioners.

It is no-brainer to say that no participants for any election should appoint the "referee" for any "match"! The writer is surprised that all the political parties in Nigeria are oblivious of this weird and strange arrangement. Can one say that they overlook it so that when they win, they too will benefit from it? This weird arrangement should be discarded if we are hoping to have free, credible, fair, peaceful elections. It does not matter how honest, truthful or saintly the Chairmen and Commissioners are or will be!

Imagine the referee in a football match being the 12th player for one side; the resultant effect is that goals will be scored either from the whistle of the referee or from his leg!

The issue of selling/buying of votes has now become our regular menu in our electoral processes. This trend is very dangerous and inimical to our democracy and electoral successes. We have a lot of work to do here. Formal education is the key! If the people are educated and have means of survival, no one will collect five to ten thousand Naira and sell his or her vote and suffer or die in four years! The money collected cannot and will not last for more than two to three days out of 365 days in the year. So, will it not be better if we vote the right candidate and survive for four years than otherwise?

To arrest this malady is very easy if our security forces and the people involved decide to act in the interest of the Nation and not for personal or regional gains. The security is not supposed to take sides. The vote-sellers and buyers are to be fished out and prosecuted.
The Civil Society groups and other monitors are doing a great job, but they should double their efforts and get special hidden cameras and drones to fish out the culprits.

The INEC, on their part, should be above board. Placing the ballot boxes in open environment which allow voters to display who they are voting for, is a means of encouraging electoral fraud!
The INEC should be truly independent and members should not belong to any registered party. The Chairman and the Commissioners should be appointed by a consortium of representatives of the Judiciary, Legislature, Media, Civil Society Groups, Women Associations, the NBA, NMA, and Society of Engineers, ASUU, among others.

COMMENTS
The Judiciary, the third arm of Government, should be held in high esteem. There are many exceptionally honest Judges/Justices, but alleged weird judgements coming from some of them, even from the Supreme Court, are concerning.
The ICPC, EFCC, Central Bank and its affiliates, Customs, Immigration, Police and other security agencies should lead the way to unearthing all possible pathways money exchanges hands. This is easier in the era of electronic money transfer. This is one of the ways to sanitise all democratic institutions.

This can best be achieved through independent bodies like the ICPC, EFCC and other security agencies. The job of tracking and monitoring cannot be effectively and efficiently done by bodies appointed by the President or Governors.

The INEC, as a body, should be truly independent as previously discussed. Watchdogging or monitoring the activities of INEC is necessary to achieve transparency and honesty.

The above is necessary to ensure credibility, integrity and neutrality of INEC as arbiter, with general acceptance and conviction that actual winner emanates from the Ballot Box and not from the COURTS!

BIBLIOGRAPHY

1.   Chinua Achebe
      "The Trouble with Nigeria"
      Published by Heinemann 1983
      ISBN 978-0-433-90698-8

2.   Briggs Daminabo Sonny
      "The Problem with Nigeria"
      Published in Nigeria, 2014
      ISBN 978-978-52709-2-1

3.   www.sahistory.org.za> article> neg
      Negotiations and the transition/South African History
      Online

4.   Medium.com> 15- inspirational quotes

5.   Martin Niemoller
      "First they came…"
      en-m.wikipedia>wiki> first_they_came

6.   The Mirror
      "Frequent fuel price hikes as dividends of Democracy"
      September 1-7, 2005
      Vol. 3, No. 36
      ISSN 1597-22 LX

7.   The Mirror
      "The many sins of the people of the Niger Delta in custody
      and in graves"
      November 11 – 16, 2005
      Vol. 3, No. 46, page 6

ISSN 1597 – 22LX

8.   The Hard Truth
        "What Nigeria needs is not constitutional amendment"
        February 23- March 1, 2006
        Vol. 7, No. 7
        ISSN 1596-2423

9.   The Hard Truth
        "The Forthcoming 2007 Elections"
        December 21-17, 2006
        Page 11

10.   The Mirror
        "Resolving the Niger Delta Crisis: What Manner of Master
        Plan?"
        July 5 – 11, 2007
        Vol 4, No. 13
        ISSN 1597 – 22LX

11.   The Hard Truth
        "How to fight corruption in Nigeria"
        October 4 -10, 2007
        Vol. 1, No. 39
        ISSN: 1596 – 2423

12.   Briggs Daminabo Sonny
        "How to fight corruption in Nigeria"
        Published in Nigeria, 2011
        ISBN: 978-978- 50186 – 6 – 0

13.   New Telegraph
        "Open letter to President-elect,

Muhammadu Buhari, on "How to fight corruption in
Nigeria"
Tuesday, May 26, 2015
Vol.2, No. 461, Back page & Page 55.

14.	Today's Topnews
"Constitutional Amendments in Nigeria – Movement
without Motion"?
Wednesday, April 6 – Tuesday, April, 12, 2022 (Weekly
tabloid)

15.	Today's Topnews
"Borrowing into the Abyss"
June 1 – 7, 2002
Vol. 21. No 2